Hollywood

Se Habla Español

**A brief glance at Hispanics in Hollywood films...
... Yesterday, today and tomorrow**

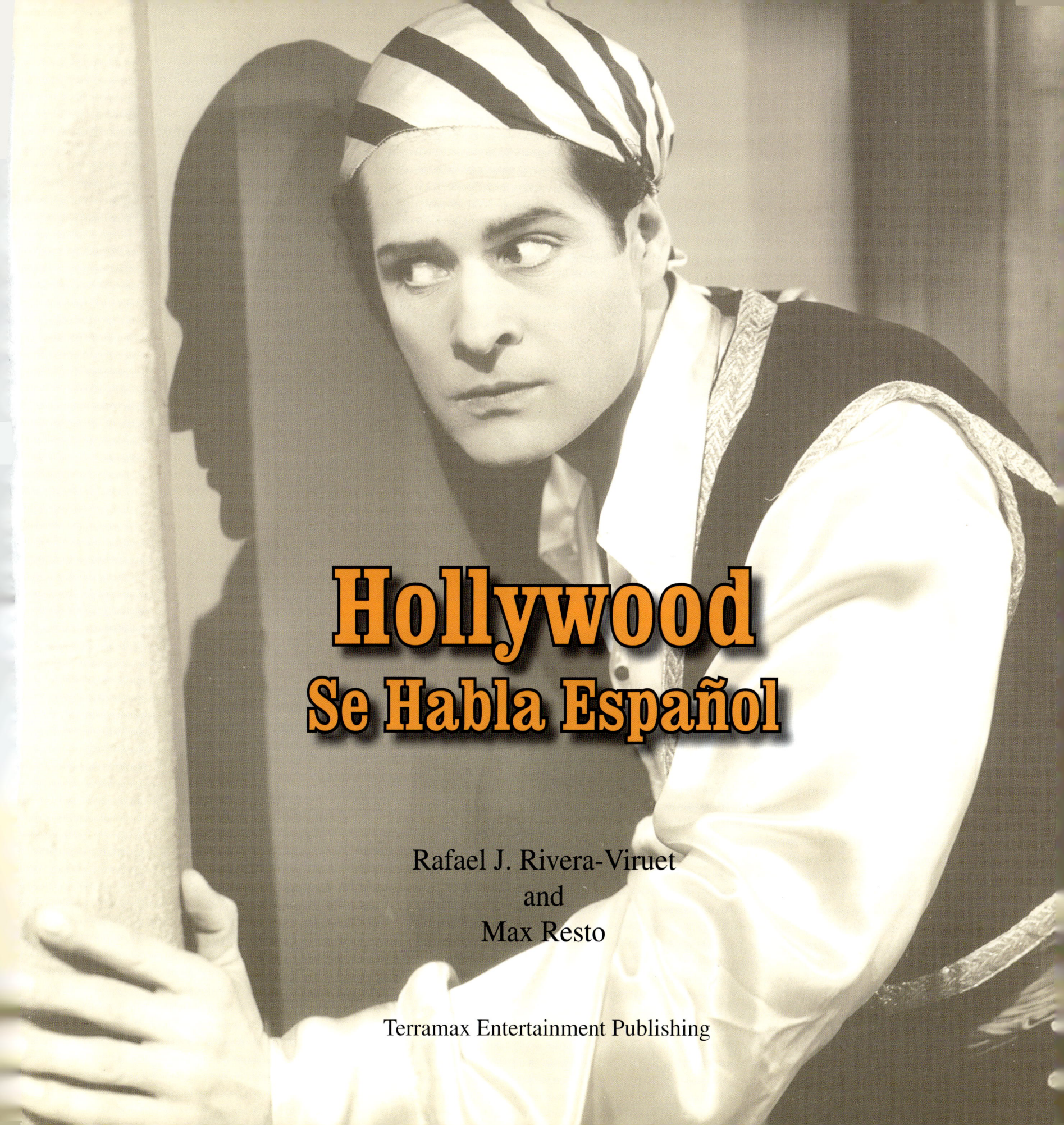

Hollywood
Se Habla Español

Rafael J. Rivera-Viruet
and
Max Resto

Terramax Entertainment Publishing

Copyright © 2008 by Rafael J. Rivera-Viruet

All the vintage images used in this book are public domain, unless noted otherwise.

All images are the sole property of their respective owners and are used here under the fair use clause of the 1976 Copyright Act.

Published by:
Terramax Entertainment Publishing
Empire State Building
350 Fifth Avenue, 59th Floor
New York, NY 10118

All rights reserved. No part of this book may be reproduced in any form, except by any newspaper, magazine or other electronic media reviewer who wishes to quote brief passages in connection with a review.

Overall Design by Max Resto based on a concept by Rafael J. Rivera-Viruet

Cover Art by:
Luis

Cover Art Chapter 5 by:
Charles Valderrama

Cover Art Chapter 6 by:
Angel "Papo" Pont

Deluxe Limited Edition

Library of Congress Cataloging-in-Publication Data

Rivera-Viruet, Rafael and Max Resto.
    Hollywood... Se Habla Español, Hispanics in Hollywood Films... Yesterday, Today and Tomorrow / by Rafael J. Rivera-Viruet and Max Resto — Deluxe Limited Edition

"A Terramax Entertainment Publishing Book."

ISBN 978-0-9816650-0-9

Table of Contents

	Acknowledgments by **Rafael J. Rivera-Viruet**	11
	Preface by **Ricardo Montalbán**	12
Chapter One:	SILENCE IS GOLDEN… The beginning of the Motion Picture industry and an international visual language is created	15
Chapter Two:	THE LATIN LOVER… The creation of an image	31
Chapter Three:	IT TALKS! … A little known chapter on the success of Hollywood Spanish-language films	53
Chapter Four:	ALLA EN EL RANCHO GRANDE… The era of the "shoot-em-ups" westerns. A film is only as good as its villain is bad	63
Chapter Five:	THE HISPANIC HOLLYWOOD HALL OF FAME… Brilliant stars who shot across the silver screen burning an everlasting image in our hearts.	83
Chapter Six:	HOLLYWOOD TODAY AND TOMORROW… The "gold rush" continues.	129
Bibliography		142
Image index		144
Map Collage 1		146
Map Collage 2		147

Opposite Page: The Little Rascals *prepare to shoot a scene in Spanish for their famous serial.*

Tittle Pages: Duncan Renaldo early in his film career.

The lovely Lupe Vélez posses for a dramatic head shot.

Acknowledgements

By Rafael J. Rivera-Viruet

The inspiration began in the early 1980s when I met a Latino "international movie star" and we both shared the same passion and vision… collecting memorabilia and telling stories of the impact that Hispanics have had in the Hollywood Cinema for the past hundred years… my biggest "thank you" to Rafael Campos.

There are so many individuals that I wish to thank and give gratitude, but it would take pages to name everyone, so to all those who contributed in one way or another to the publication of this book … muy agradecido… it took over 25 years to complete.

I remember sharing this dream, back then, with Alex Colón, Esther Freifeld, Ismael Carlo, Héctor Elizondo, Miriam Colón, Perry López, Henry Silva and Eva Montealegre… I was encouraged by the young Latino talent that I met like: Edward James Olmos, Esaí Morales, Elizabeth Peña, Robert Beltrán, Jimmy Smits, Lillian Hurst, Ramón Franco, Wanda de Jesús, Tony Plana, Benicio Del Toro and many more.

Maestro Ricardo Montalbán, who has dedicated his life to improving the image of the Hispanic community. His introduction is appreciated beyond words.

Marc Wanamaker and my compatriot Javier Santiago, creator of La Fundación para la Cultura Popular in Puerto Rico, for their generosity in sharing their fantastic collection of vintage images and original prints.

Every writer needs to be edited to expand on the vision of what one is trying to write, so I thank Gilbert Rivera, Tim Cusack, Joseph Zwerling and Michael Quixote Fellmeth for their enthusiasm.

Fernando Campos, publisher of Canales Magazine. The moral support of Efraín Logreira, Jerry Velasco, the NOSOTROS organization, Stella Bustos, Stephen Sultan, Jesús García, Vicky Figueroa Vidal and my advertising gurus: Judy Korman Sultan and Rodd Rodríguez. Tony and Esther Velázquez, who have been my angels and John Badillo, whom I have known forever. My children Denise, Andy, Taína Maya, Rafael and my wonderful partner in life, Elizabeth Figueroa, who continues to motivate and inspire me.

My mother Domitila "Tinita" Viruet, who taught us the power of the written word, and my dearest brother Col. A. M. "Andy" Rivera (USAF, Ret.) for his love and support in all my endeavors.

I could not have finished this long journey without the collaboration of my dear friend and writing partner, the very talented Marcelino "Max" Resto.

Gracias a todos y cada uno.

Preface

More than a hundred years ago, when the moving pictures were introduced to the world, I'm willing to bet the inventors, as well as all those pioneers of filmmaking, did not suspect the profound way this new media was going to influence society.

The perfect mixture of pure science and the fancy of the creative world, the phenomenon of capturing images on film and then simply project them on a white canvas screen, definitely revolutionized the way people were to seek entertainment from that time forth.

Indulging in an art form that imitates life, life itself in a magical combination with the boundless nature of the imagination to become the material for great art, the moving picture opened the door to a whole universe of creative possibilities. A great venue to a wide diversity of disciplines, acting included (but not by any means exclusive) the saga of taking a film project all the way to that white canvas is a humbling task, regardless of the part played in the process.

Filled with myths and legends... in Hollywood, this complex movie mecca, the stories abound... Fabulous stories well worth telling and with the Latino presence as a constant and important subject.

Thus the importance of the tome now in your hands: *Hollywood... Se Habla Español* is a document that takes pride in the Latino contribution to the film industry, celebrates our presence in this important media and provides us with a way of keeping track of were we come from, so it becomes easier to wisely decide were we want to go...

Technology keeps improving and continues to influence our taste... For better or worse, who knows?... The sets are more elaborate and the players often-times shift in a dazzling succession of bright luminaries, yet history keeps unfolding and it is so easy to lose track, obliviously shunning those who paved the way, taught us the most valuable lessons, defined the industry and obviously set the standards.

I applaud Rafael Rivera-Viruet and Max Resto for their years of research and commitment. It is with great delight that I embrace this effort to shine the spotlight on the Latinos that at one time were making the headlines alongside the ones making headlines today, a long awaited and remarkable endeavor.

The Hispanic Hollywood Hall of Fame will undoubtedly be the source of great pride and the best motivator for people from all walks of life and ethnic backgrounds, this Latino presence commands a place in history and calls to be submitted to closer scrutiny and serious consideration as it is done here.

Hollywood... Se Habla Español is a deserving homage to the Latino figure, placing it in its right historical context and, in an entertaining way, detailing their contributions. How joyful it is to have all those memories, all those faces, friends, colleagues and associates, all this beautiful and big Latino family gathered in one place, and ready to be cherished now and forever.

Ricardo Montalbán

Chapter 1

SILENCE IS GOLDEN...

The beginning of the Motion Picture Industry

When Thomas Alva Edison, the famous early 20th century inventor, was working on a new combination of alloys for an automobile steel axle, one of the ways he used to illustrate the strength of his latest creation was to test it with an unprecedented stunt and record it on film.

"We must have a car crash," was his request, "Over a cliff."

So, Edison's special steel axle is installed in a new car, and the whole thing is sent over a cliff as requested, in Palisades, New Jersey. The subsequent head-on crash makes for a memorable scene, the footage showing how the improved steel part is strong enough to withstand the strain of the great impact and the fire that ensues.

The film was released on August 27, 1909, and the critics raved: "... makes one sit up and take notice."

Thus, the creation of the one-reel drama.

The film had a car race that ends in a spectacular disaster. "The Duke's machine plunges down a precipice, exploding and taking fire as it goes, enveloping its occupant in a blinding cloud of smoke and steam. The action is so natural that it seems as though the accident really occurred." Edison had taken the first step toward what modern-day productions routinely do in movies like *Die Hard* and *The Terminator*.

That early attempt at realism and drama set a new standard for special effects in film by a man who took only a passing interest in filmmaking. At the time one of this country's more fascinating personalities, Thomas Alva Edison, and against dissident opinions, was not Hispanic.

From the onset, melodrama was the primary ingredient of the silent film.

The exact date and who created the celluloid, the flexible and highly light sensitive material that made moving pictures a reality, is also the subject of much discussion, colliding hypotheses and data.

During its early stages, when the new and exciting media was introduced to audiences during the late 19th century, the film camera was used exclusively and unflinchingly to record simple everyday occurrences: people at a train station, an animated street scene, etc. It was some time before the disciplines of editing and creative camera work began to peek from within the folds of this new and promising form of recording history and communicating with an audience.

In 1898 this new art form began to take shape with *Cripple Creek Bar Room*, a four-minute film that started what was to become a national myth: the Western. Melodramas, comedies and Westerns were the main fare for those early nickelodeon audiences. As expected, the players who embodied these life depictions were either good-looking or great characters. Charles Chaplin and Buster Keaton took full advantage of their talent as actors and comedians trained for the stage, and in front of the film camera, their antics became iconographic of this era. Relying

Poster art for Maré Nostrum, *a Silent Era gem where two Latino names stand out: Antonio Moreno as the male lead and Blasco Ibáñez, the famed Spanish author.*

Title Page: Duncan Renaldo circa the Silent Era.

Romance, the silent love story full of fantasy and mysticism where anything is possible, took the audiences on lasting voyages of passion and boundless treks of the imagination.

on their innate ability for some very entertaining physical comedy, which still amazes and entertains audiences up to this day, the two of them took the screen by storm and imprinted the cultural panorama with some indelible performances, redefining the media and its possibilities for decades to come.

Silent pictures, and their inventive way of looking at the nuances of love, comedy, drama and adventure, soon became a mainstay of modern life, which prompted filmmakers to sink their teeth into all these marketable themes and subjects.

Romance, the silent love story full of fantasy and mystery where anything is possible, took the audiences on lasting voyages of passion and boundless treks of the imagination. Without voices and ordinary sounds, the hidden intents and, most important, the emotional ties binding the love-struck characters were even more present in those images flashing at 24 frames per second on the canvas of the screen. The new media grew, taking a strong hold of audiences and maintaining a tight grip on those always hungering for the escapist stories of dashing heroes, heated love affairs, and incredible, larger-than-life adventures.

The very first film studios were established in sheds and warehouses. In 1908 Edison held court in the Bronx, while American Vitagraph Company set its facilities in Flatbush, and Biograph, the oldest film-producing company, was on 14th Street in New York City. Silig Essanay, another early day, film producing endeavor, set up its studios in Chicago.

These companies, along with five others, in 1909 founded the Motion Picture Patents Co. (MPPC), claiming the exclusive right to photograph, print and develop motion pictures.

Many felt that the MPPC was an elitist group that wanted to monopolize the industry. Some said the companies of MPPC had little tendency toward the artistic development of film and were "concerned solely with gouging every possible dollar out of trade."

Distributors such as Carl Laemmle of the Laemmle Film Service soon put an end to that. He fought the monopoly, in court and out. He ridiculed the MPPC in trade press and produced his own movies. The Laemmle family is still responsible for creating and distributing rare films of artistry that make a statement. Despite all the controversy over who invented what or who had control of this or that patent, the silent movie grew in popularity. The film industry caught on like wild fire.

House magazines, soon to become fan magazines, started in 1912. They provided listings of current and forthcoming films, nurturing vast public interest. Beauty hints and fashion notes became an important aspect of the fan magazine. Women learned how to "beautify their skin intelligently." "Charming" costumes designed for Mary Pickford were featured. Every lady wanted to know what it took to be a glamorous beauty. Ads promised one could "grow eyebrows and eyelashes" like the stars. Actor Warren William was quoted as saying "Only the Natural Lips appeal to me." Often, actresses were pitted against each other, i.e., GARBO VS. DIETRICH.

Articles featured "Chaplin's New Contract" in reference to his marital status. "Movy-Dols,"

One of the Silent Era's biggest star was the beautiful and talented Dolores Del Río.

Ramón Novarro (in the tub) and Edward Everett Horton in a scene from The Night is Young.

little paper cutouts of the stars, were sold through these magazines. Gossip columns were born. In this way, public interest in, and acceptance of the stars began to have its influence. Artists named as top money-makers in the *Motion Picture Herald* could experience something akin to winning an Oscar today. People began to look to the stars as a sort of aristocracy. Movie performers did set the trends of the time, vogue actions by the always shining stars that would be reflected by the general public, mainly in dress and attitudes, even mores.

Ever since the creation of the North American filmmaking industry, Hispanics have held an important and influential place within its movie-producing machinery. Yet, creating a reliable map of that influence and the undeniable contributions made by artists, actors, screenwriters and technicians of Latin descent proves to be like putting together a complicated puzzle, one made up of many, many pieces, most of them missing or misplaced among the very complicated structure of the studio system, the current corporate models and even the ever-present independent film producers.

From the very beginning of the moving picture industry, the whole creative endeavor was widely populated by many talented, handsome, engaging and always-present figures, coming from all walks of life.

While many Anglo artists started to shine and sparkle, adorning the film star constellation with names of undeniable appeal and talent, coupled with very strong and constant screen presences, it comes as no surprise that alongside the names of Clara Bow, Mary Pickford, Victor McLaglen, Edmund Lowe, and even Chaplin and Keaton, were also Dolores Del Río, Antonio Moreno, Ramón Novarro and so many others. Proud of their Hispanic heritage, they also took on the labor of bringing to life the fantasies meant for the golden screen.

> *"I prefer to live my novels rather than to write them."*
>
> ***Vicente Blasco Ibáñez***
> ***Spanish novelist and screenwriter***

Vicente Blasco Ibáñez, a Victorian novelist and Spanish national, was an established screenwriter during the silent period of the Hollywood movie-making industry.

During the glorious period of the silent screen, Vicente Blasco Ibáñez, a Victorian novelist and Spanish national, was an established screenwriter in Hollywood. A writer with great influence in film, the public's image of Latinos, and life in general, as well as an impressive artist, the prolific Blasco Ibáñez was once quoted as saying, "I prefer to live my novels rather than to write them."

Beside publishing international titles like *Maré Nostrum* and other famous works of fiction, he is credited with penning some of Spain's finest regional novels and was even considered for a Nobel Prize in literature.

Blasco Ibáñez, who wrote the film script for *Maré Nostrum,* as well as for his other novel *Blood and Sand*, also wrote the now famous and immortal novel *The Four Horsemen of the Apocalypse*, which in 1921 was adapted for the silver screen by screenwriter June Mathis and became a Rudolph Valentino vehicle (more on him later). The debonair artist was jailed in his youth, hunted and exiled by the Spanish monarch, and fought in six bloody duels. He single-handedly battled the entrenched Spanish monarch, the Fascist party and the Catholic Church. A strategist, propagandist, financier and soldier, he once hired pilots and planes to fly over the cities of Spain and drop anti-fascist pamphlets. Never since have we had such a herculean writer to tell the Latino story.

Antonio Moreno (at left) and David Torrence in Her Husband's Secret.

Antonio Moreno was another important character from those early years of film production. His father was a noncommissioned officer in the Spanish army and his mother was from a socially prominent family in Spain. Moreno worked for a time as a sweeper and tester for a New England telephone company. He was also a meter reader for a light company and a jewelry store salesman. Finally, he moved toward theatre and film. Moreno's first stage appearance was in 1912 in a small part in *A Little Minister*. His first film was *Voice of the Millions*, also a small part. He performed in *Judith of Bethulia, The Invisible Hand, The Perils of Thunder Mountain, Two Daughters of Eve, So Near Yet So Far,* and the *House of Discord*, all filmed in 1914. The next year he worked in *Too Many Husbands, The Loan Shark King,* and *The Peacemaker*. Later he did *Gypsy Trail*, participated in D.W. Griffith's *Birth of A Nation* and also appeared in *The Lonesome Pine*.

Widely known as the man who could create a heat that would register 110 degrees in the shade, Ramón Novarro went on to solidify the image of the Latin lover (more on that later) and to star in many films that made his name shine with the same intensity as his Anglo counterparts. *Prisoner of Zenda*, a movie directed by the important filmmaker Rex Ingram, put Novarro in the foreground of the business. Many remakes have been done of this film, but none have been as successful as this first dramatic effort.

In Hollywood, Novarro had a famous second cousin, Dolores Del Río. Described as "orchidaceous," the stunning Latina beauty hailed from Durango, but she was not a poor aspiring actress facing all kinds of hardship to attain fame and fortune. Del Río, instead, was a well-to-do Mexican *señorita*, the daughter of a bank president, married at 16 to Jaime Del Río, a wealthy Mexican businessman.

It was Edwin Carewe, a film director from the United States, who discovered the Mexican beauty while on a trip with his wife to Mexico City. While attending a wedding in the Mexican capital, they met the Del Ríos at a tea party. One look at Dolores and Carewe was taken by the outgoing and delightfully beautiful young Latina. Before his return to Hollywood, Carewe gave her a small part in *Joanna*. The 1925 film project was her first appearance in front of the camera and was soon followed in 1926 with *Highsteppers* and then *Pal*. She was loaned to Universal for an Edward Everett Horton film, *The Whole Town's Talking*. Then Fox borrowed her for *What Price Glory*, starring Edmund Lowe and Victor McLaglen. This film banked a reported two millions dollars, a record at that time. Dolores played the seductive Charmain.

Described as "orchidaceous," the stunning Latina beauty Dolores Del Río was a well-to-do Mexican señorita, the daughter of a bank president, married at 16 to a wealthy Mexican businessman.

In *Resurrection*, filmed in 1927, Dolores performed the role of Katyusha Maslova, considered one of her best performances, opposite Rod La Rocque, a famous movie star of the time, who played Prince Dimitri. That same year she also starred in *The Loves of Carmen* under the direction of Raoul Walsh. Another Latino, Don Alvarado played Don José, while Victor McLaglen embodied the part of Escamillo.

Del Río is on record as saying: "Nevair, nevair, will I make a talkie. I zink zey are tairibble." Some thought she wouldn't go over as big once sound was introduced, because of her accent. But she did make talkies and went on to enjoy a long and fruitful career in film.

Above: Dolores Del Río in the midst of a love scene.

Opposite Page: Lupe Vélez.

Later Dolores divorced her husband and married director Cedric Gibbons in 1930. She divorced Gibbons in 1941. Dolores held onto her flaming beauty throughout her career. She was seen frequently in the company of Orson Welles, who had admired her from afar for many years. He directed her in the film *Journey Into Fear* in 1942.

Del Río, a smart woman, signed a contract that gave her a percentage of the profits from her screen performances, enabling her to enjoy a comfortable retirement. She would return to Hollywood thereafter only for films that she felt merited her talent, such as the mythical *Children of Sánchez*, during the 1970s. Del Río was one of the first Latinas to merit the title of screen diva and was long celebrated for her outstanding beauty and undeniable talent.

Comedy was just the beginning for the energetic Lupe Vélez. Known for her laughter in spite of the fact that she was strapped with family responsibilities due to the illness of her father, she always seemed able to find joy in life. Known in Mexico as "The Wild Girl," her first English words were "banana split" and "go to hell." In a snap, United Artists signed her to a five-year contract.

Whether in short bobbed curls, long braids or draped in scarves, Lupe Vélez was a stunning beauty with an uncanny sense of humor.

Lupe was good friends with Fannie Brice, a stage star at the time. When Vélez tested for the screen, her gusto for life proved fortuitous. Douglas Fairbanks took one look at her zestful screen test and said, "Sign her!" Thus, she became the female lead in his film, *The Gaucho*.

The critics raved about *The Gaucho* and about Vélez: "In Lupe Vélez, Douglas Fairbanks has for the first time a female partner in his antics. She is fully spirited as he, sliding down ropes, leaping onto horses and fighting." She was pretty handy with a knife, too. The role made her famous. The picture takes place in the "city of the miracle visions of the Virgin Mary," where a little girl first sets eyes on the famous gaucho, played by Fairbanks. Years later, there's a 10,000-peso reward for the capture of the Gaucho. Now, the little girl has grown up, and she has a crush on the Gaucho like no other. He couldn't get rid of her if he wanted to! And he doesn't want to. When he wrapped a rope around the two of them, the audience witnessed an erotic tango-like dance between Fairbanks and Vélez that foreshadowed a legendary real-life love affair.

Thereafter, audiences often saw Vélez as tempestuous, temperamental leads, notably in D. W. Griffith's *Lady of the Pavements*. Whether in short bobbed curls, long braids or draped in scarves, Lupe Vélez was a stunning beauty with an uncanny sense of humor. She was a blazing torch, a firebrand, plus she was funny! In the *Wolf Song*, a pagan call to wanderlust, Lupe Vélez is a woman of love. Gary Cooper, who actually had an affair with Lupe in real

Above right: Lupe Vélez and a typical Hollywood "bad guy."

Opposite page: Dubbed The Mexican Spitfire, Lupe Vélez's gusto for life was fortuitous.

When famed actor and producer Douglas Fairbanks took one look at Lupe Vélez's zestful screen test, he just said, "Sign her!"

"In Lupe Vélez I find a girl who takes the same joy out of primitive, elemental things that I do. I have found that the most casual linking of our names causes dynamite."

Gary Cooper
Hollywood Star

---

life, is her new hombre. *Wolf Song*, a Paramount release, was the first musical film romance and Cooper was exceptionally attractive as a "natural" man. The hair-dressers had to work all day keeping his hair rumpled. News got out that Lupe and Gary were doing more than just a film together, and this fanned the flames of Lupe's reputation as a "hot tamale."

It was said that pleasant vocalizing permeated the film. Gary Cooper plays a man who loves 'em and leaves 'em until he meets up with Vélez! A picturesque production, it was a Western designed for more than just the usual masculine appeal. There were several scenes of great majestic beauty.

Photoplay's Evaline Lieber wrote of Vélez: "How well I remember the day Lupe Vélez heard a rumor... that Gary Cooper and his leading lady were interested in each other. Lupe went to location... She could hold her man against any competition when she's on the set... Gary didn't have a chance to remember whether the lips he was kissing for the screen were those of a live girl or a mummy. He was thinking of Lupe." It was later reported that Vélez and Cooper were driving people from the hills (the Hollywood Hills) with raucous arguments. Cooper was quoted as saying: "In Lupe Vélez I find a girl who takes the same joy out of primitive, elemental things that I do. I have found that the most casual linking of our names causes dynamite."

Though few believed that Vélez would be able to continue her career after the introduction of sound, she did. She was quite successful in *The Mexican Spitfire*. She was not so successful in love, which caused her despair. After so many years of creating laughter and excitement for countless audiences, she committed suicide at the young age of 36 in her flower-bedecked room.

Either as the lover, the villain or the fool, Latin men and women were present during those early sparks of brilliance in the rich moving pictures constellation that was the heyday of the Hollywood star system. A contribution well deserving of being highlighted, praised and thoroughly documented, their work fed a flame that took off like wildfire and helped give the silver screen the luster, importance and profits it enjoys up to this day.

The Latin persona is perfect for conveying many engaging emotions and telling many a full and enjoyable story on screen. The Latino image has enjoyed a long-term love affair with the camera, one that remains alive and well after more than a hundred years of movie-making. Those silent gems spoke to our innermost being without ever saying a word or making a sound, but they established in very clear terms the undeniable fact that even during that silent era, Hollywood from its very beginnings always had a sign that read "Se habla Español."

Chapter 2

THE LATIN LOVER
The creation of an image

During the early years of silent films, the lead players were predominantly Anglo. A Latin male playing the hero, lead character or lover was a rare occurrence. But with the arrival of Rudolph Valentino, that changed overnight.

The young rising star, who was of Italian descent, and whose real name was Rodolfo Alfonzo Raffaelo Pierre Filibert Guglielmi di Valentina d'Antonguolla, was cast in the leading role in 1921's *The Four Horsemen of Apocalypse*, under the dexterous hand of director Rex Ingram.

This film offered a romanticized view of the many dimensions of the Latin male, making the Latino image into a fashionable trend, especially with a female audience, throngs of avid fans would flock to theaters every time the marquee announced a new romantic venture with the dark and handsome Valentino. This new image of a strong, oftentimes cruel, yet passionate and, most important, exotic character was one that producers and studios were determined to run with and milk for all it was worth.

Many historians feel it was Ingram, whose career began after an encouraging meeting with Charles Edison, son of the inventor, was the one who actually created the image that made Valentino such a huge success. He had worked eight years as a director before the formidable success of *The Four Horsemen of Apocalypse*. As a director, Ingram would continue to have a major impact on silent film and the Latin image.

Producers and studios recognized a great well of possibilities for the Latin lover in film. Inspired by the financial success of this romantic-slash-macho image, studios began to search for scripts that presented Latin characters of depth and complexity.

Only some old, very old fans, movie enthusiasts and a handful of film scholars remember Rex Ingram and the important part he played in the development of the art of filmmaking, by this point, most everybody has been exposed to the legend of Valentino one way or another.

The charismatic actor had a special way with women and with the public in general. At the time of his death, the suicides of several women were reported that were attributed to his demise. And even the famed 20th century psychic, George B. Wehner, made a career for himself by relaying messages from the "spirit" of Valentino.

Quoted as saying that "a love affair with a stupid person is like a cold cup of coffee," and that "the greatest asset to a woman is dignity," Valentino was also credited with some inspiring pieces of metaphor such as "love is honey. It is a flower. It may be fierce as a tiger lily, but it must be beautiful, delicate, gentle too." He said his most treasured moments were "when a gentle, loving sigh opened the treasure house of a woman's heart and she spoke truly of those things within." Valentino was also quoted as saying that there were no movies in heaven because "films are a mechanical perversion of the drama."

The Latin lover of the screen was exotic, sexy and sometimes a little cruel in his ardor. It's interesting to note that the men who played these Latin lovers on the screen were often reputed to be gentle and gracious in real life. These admirable qualities must have radiated from the actors to create a devoted audience of women who lived and died in the light that came from the image on the screen.

Rudolph Valentino added momentum to the movement of Latin men in film, but he was not the only Latin lover and certainly not the first. The Spaniard Antonio Moreno was a famed screen actor when Valentino was still working as a bus boy.

A documented Latin lover in real life, Moreno played suitor to a number of great actresses during his time: Norma Talmadge, Blanche Sweet, Edith Storey, Pearl White, Bebe Daniels, Agnes Ayres, Mary Miles Minter, Gloria Swanson, Pola Negri,

Rodolfo Alfonzo Raffaelo Pierre Filibert Guglielmi di Valentina d'Antonguolla or, simply put, Rudolph Valentino.

> *"Like a Spanish cavalier I would gladly prostrate myself
> on the street so she could step on me. Look at her, a woman
> admired and adored by everyone.
> And what am I? Nothing but a poor motion picture actor."*
>
> ***Antonio Moreno,***
> ***after he married oil heiress Daisy Canfield.***

Rene Adoree, Dorothy Gish, Irene Castle, Alice Terry, Marion Davies and Greta Garbo, the list is long, all of them were shining luminaries within the Hollywood constellation of stars, and all connected at one time or another to the hot and handsome Latino heartthrob. At that time, Moreno could have had his pick.

"Like a Spanish cavalier I would gladly prostrate myself on the street so she could step on me," said Moreno, known for his engaging modesty, after he married the lovely and popular oil heiress Daisy Canfield. "Look at her, a woman admired and adored by everyone. And what am I? Nothing but a poor motion picture actor."

Speaking of love in silent films, he stated that "no leading man would dare stand with arms sticking out of his shoulders and speak words of love." Like many actors of the silent film era, Moreno was disdainful of the new acting style that came with the "talkie." Unhappy with the advent of sound, he felt that spoken words betrayed the true emotion.

Each step of Moreno's career was a careful one. Having begun at the onset of film, he was an expert, a veteran. Though his dark good looks were an asset, he was not always cast as a Latino. In 1921 *Her Husband's Secret* was marketed as: "Bankers! Divorce! Fraud! Suicide!" National produced

Mauritz Stiller (left) directs Greta Garbo and Antonio Moreno.

Opposite Page: Handsome Antonio Moreno posses for a head shot.

this in the pre-flapper days, and Moreno plays a somber, handsome, clean-cut character who goes to a wild party and who's life subsequently becomes unraveled.

The Spanish Dancer, a Paramount film released in 1923, stars Moreno as a lovable and dashing devil-may-care character. Moreno grew a chin beard for this part written by June Mathis from the play *Don César de Bazán*. Mathis had also written the screenplay for the towering success *The Four Horsemen of the Apocalypse*, which continued to hold box office records until the release of *Gone With The Wind* in 1939.

Moreno and the great actress Bebe Daniels, also of Latin descent (more on her later), made an exotic, handsome couple in *The Exciters* for Paramount. They were also cast in *Tiger Love* —based on *El Gato Montés* (*The Wildcat*), a story of hot Castilian love. The film, a Spanish Robin Hood tale, is at its best when the character played by Moreno holds up a gambling hall and then kidnaps the heroine on her wedding day during a splendid rain scene. Moreno cuts a fine figure as the bandit, lover and hero. Given that the Robin Hood role is a great vehicle for any actor (to hold a woman tenderly, to fight courageously and still be a rascal is the ultimate multidimensional portrayal), Moreno took full advantage of this opportunity to strengthen his hold on the moviegoers of that time.

In 1926, Moreno starred in *Maré Nostrum* in what some consider to be his biggest movie hit. Alice Terry, who declared it her favorite film, played his love interest. Filmed on location in Spain and Italy and based on the novel by Blasco Ibáñez, the movie was directed by Ingram.

Antonio Moreno (at left) shows his acting skills during this silent scene.

Opposite Page:
Poster art for The Temptress, *a block-buster of its time.*

The year is 1926, MGM is the studio and The Temptress *is the new film project. But, most important, it was Moreno and Greta Garbo.*

The year is 1926, MGM is the studio, and *The Temptress* is the new film project. But, most important, the actors are Moreno and Greta Garbo. In another Blasco Ibáñez creation, Garbo plays a woman of sinister passion and Moreno, the hero. A masquerade ball in Paris starts the story, but a cruel duel with whips soon ensues. Moreno initially refused to shave a moustache he was sporting at the time, but finally agreed to, as requested by director Maurice Stiller. He was originally billed above Garbo, until the diva objected. The production was plagued with troubles from the beginning. Finally MGM's genius Irving Thalberg saw fit to fire Stiller, Garbo's mentor. This enraged the diva. In his place, a young, dynamic and talented Fred Niblo was appointed as director. The movie was completed and made its debut to raging reviews: "a fundamental fire was sparked and it burns every time."

Niblo, who began as a successful blackface performer (who was often requested by royalty), had a close working relationship with Blasco Ibáñez. They worked together on several different projects and were well matched. Niblo also directed *Blood and Sand*, from a Blasco Ibáñez' novel, *Camille*, *Ben Hur*, *The Three Musketeers* and *The Mark of Zorro*, to name a few.

The year Moreno worked with Niblo on *The Temptress*, he was arrested and jailed while visiting his native Spain. Charged with carrying a pistol and consorting with extremists, he managed to escape execution in spite of these accusations.

In 1926 MGM featured Moreno in *The Flaming Forest*, a glorified Western. The most riveting scenes were an Indian attack and a forest fire. Moreno played a sergeant in the Northwest Mounties, Canada's famed police.

Then he was the star of the sensational screen version of *It* in 1927 opposite another silver screen darling, Clara Bow. People went crazy over the "blatant" sensuality and the steamy scenes between the two, making this film Paramount Studio's most popular movie that year. This role transformed Bow into the ultimate flapper and the embodiment of sensuality, a sex symbol of the roaring twenties

Still not happy about the end of the Silent Era, Antonio said: "I'd love to see Hollywood toss the spoken word out the window..." A big-time domino player, he originated the fashionable pastime in Hollywood. His last film was *The Searchers* in 1956, and he died at the age of 80 on February 15, 1967. He was one of the few stars that Paramount very rarely loaned to other companies. His talent was irrefutable from the very inception of film and ever present throughout his career.

Though many expected Latin lovers of the screen to be bitter rivals, this was seldom the case. However, directors and actors sometimes found themselves building their careers dependant on one another, creating on the set a tense atmosphere of competition. Audiences benefited from these mostly frivolous ego contests, which always wound up in the gossip pages of fanzines and periodicals. This created the necessity to provide a forum for several Latinos to grace the screen with their ultra-macho, passionate-lover personae, dark and handsome, oftentimes mustachioed (rarely seen before in Hollywood unless you played the bad guy), with diverse qualities to choose from.

Dolores Del Río poses for the still camera during her silent screen years.

Ramón Novarro in a dramatic silent scene.

Amidst one of these minor industry skirmishes, Valentino left Metro, causing Ingram to lose his leading man to another studio. But the savvy director, still clinging to the suave and debonair qualities of the Latino leading man, selected Ramón Samaniegos, a handsome Mexican youth who was as an extra in *The Four Horsemen of Apocalypse*, to fulfill this role under his wise tutelage. Under lngram's guidance he became Ramón Novarro, the new Latin lover for Ingram's films and a new Latino star for the whole world to praise and adore.

In 1922, Ingram directed Novarro in *Trifling Woman*, co-starring Barbara La Marr, a silent-screen star of controversial sensuality cast several times opposite hot Latin men. Originally titled *Black Orchids*, the American Film Institute describes this romantic drama with few words: Novelists.... Fatherhood.... Infidelity.... Paris... Chimpanzees...

Some state that Novarro's biggest break came in 1923 with the film *Scaramouche*. Based on a popular novel by Rafael Sabantini, this project was also directed by Ingram. Metro presented this drama of an uprising in an unhappy town that occurs following a fiery speech by Scaramouche, the character portrayed by the young and extremely handsome Novarro. Wigs, foppish clothing and beautiful carriages made up the props and setting. Alice Terry, Ingram's wife at the time, played Novarro's love interest.

In another stroke of genius from Ingram, Novarro and Terry, again as his female opposite, worked in front of the camera with native Algerians in *The Arab* (1924), a true-to-life drama. With more-than-convincing performances, the duo of actors are just as believable as the natives. *The Arab* was considered at the time to be a "sex" movie, but not without some veritable scholastic merit. The drama, scenery, atmosphere and high-art photography were reported as perfection. A July 16 review of the film in Variety described *The Arab* as the "finest sheik film of them all. *The Arab* is a compliment to the screen, a verification of the sterling repute of Rex Ingram, and withal a sure financial hit."

Thy Name Is Woman, directed by Niblo and produced by Metro, broke records when it was immediately booked in over 100 theatres throughout the country, the beginning of the wide-distribution practice. A tragedy taking place amongst the mountains of Spain, Novarro plays a trooper with a mission of seduction. Barbra La Marr portrays the wife of the top smuggler in the country, the woman our hero is supposed to seduce. William V. Mong plays the elderly but clever culprit whom the woman betrays. The sex was permitted to run wild between Novarro and La Marr. The wife was described as "a woman with hands like flame and skin as soft as silk." There is also a fantastic storm scene.

Opposite Page: Ramón Novarro in the famous chariot scene from Ben Hur.

Below Right: Poster art for Scaramouche.

Motion picture box office history was established in 1926 with the still-famous *Ben Hur,* film by MGM. After all the years since its debut, *Ben Hur* remains an awesome and moving religious spectacle. Novarro plays the young Jerusalem nobleman under oppressive Roman rule. This film is a spectacle, an epic classic in the complete sense of that term. The book had already been a best seller, and this silent version is reported to be one of the most successful of all pre-talkie films.

After agreeing to not show the character of Christ in the film, June Mathis, the successful writer and a studio power broker, wrote the screen treatment. She chose the cast and hired director Charles Brabin to be at the head of the shooting, but Brabin's footage

was awful and he was replaced by Niblo. It was at this point that the handsome, young and talented Novarro took over as the new Ben Hur.

Filming began on location in Italy, where enthusiasm almost turned into tragedy. During the filming of a sea battle, Italian fisherman stood by in boats to pick up members of the company as they dropped into the water. Hungry locals, who had agreed to do extra work for the money, claiming they could swim, couldn't and nearly drowned.

The chariot scene was risky business as well. Conditions under the action director, the rather sadistic Reaves Eason, had crew members complaining about the death of 100 horses. When a stuntman was killed, a return to Hollywood was ordered. Well, Culver City, to be exact!

The chariot race and an incredibly filmed sea battle made the film a dangerous venture and later a raving success. Niblo honored the agreement and only showed the hand of Christ.

The authentic sets, costumes and racy outfits for the stars were extraordinary, even by today's standards. *Ben Hur* took two years to produce and is still known as the Wonder Movie. More money was spent on this film than any other until the *Gone With the Wind* phenomena. The daring love scenes between Novarro and his female counterpart spice up the plot, and the breathtaking action sequences tantalize audiences, creating a timeless and complete film experience.

Next, Novarro was paired with the astonishing beauty, Norma Sherer as they pay tribute to young love in 1927's *The Student Prince in Old Heidelberg*. Novarro plays an heir to the throne who must give up his love for a tavern maid because of duty to his country. Objecting to the use of makeup as heavy-handed, rabid fans stated that Novarro's looks were quite good on their own.

Paired again with Alice Terry, *Lovers?*, a film directed by John M. Stahl and produced by MGM, featured Novarro as the young José. His elderly guardian, an aging diplomat, marries the younger dame Felicia (Terry), and all hell breaks loose as the two young birds fall in love. There's a terrible duel, and the lovers take off on a ship bound for Argentina.

The Pagan, a film dabbling with the contrast between an idyllic tropical haven played against the

Above Greta Garbo and Ramón Novarro in a scene from Mata Hari.

Facing page: Ramón Novarro

> *"The leading man is always handsome in Hollywood. And the leading lady is always a pretty one. In Europe, there is more individuality ... fat men, thin men and unattractive men play the leads. They are chosen because they are human and appealing, and not for looks alone."*
>
> ***Ramón Novarro***
> ***regarding his work in Europe***

cruel realities of modern economics, approaches delicate ethnic questions with high entertainment and dramatic flair. This 1929 MGM production with several song sequences is rare in that Novarro sings. Sensational on-location photography is supported by a fine assemblage of other attractive production values. The film features Novarro as a simple, kind lover, wearing only a sheer scarf around his hips through most of the movie. The rest of the time, he is naked. This makes for very realistic, hot and sexy scenes. There is an enthralling love scene with Novarro and Dorothy Janis in front of a waterfall. A hypocritical white trader, excellently portrayed by Donald Crisp, provides the dramatic counterpart.

With some good performances from the supporting cast and acknowledged as having outstanding photography featuring beautiful tropical landscapes, the film is also filled with fine singing. Peel a banana, get a coconut from that tree, lets sing and make merry; that could convert one to paganism in a flash.

But, the mini-scarf-donning Novarro was a devout Catholic, who sang in the choir at Our Lady of Guadalupe Church in Los Angeles. In 1940 he fled from Italy, where he was working, just before Mussolini joined up with Hitler in the war against the allies. When asked how he became known as such a silent sizzler in his Latin lover heyday, he said, "I did it with a look."

Regarding his work in Europe, Novarro said: "the leading man is always handsome in Hollywood. And the leading lady is always a pretty one. In Europe, there is more individuality ... fat men, thin men and unattractive men play the leads. They are chosen because they are human and appealing, and not for looks alone."

Still handsome in his fifties, Novarro had a big comeback in RKO's *The Big Steal* with Jane Greer. He was murdered on Halloween night in 1968, his seventieth year. Paul Ferguson, a 22-year-old robber, and his teenage brother, Tom, only seventeen, were convicted of the crime. It was reported that they beat the movie star to death with his own ivory-handle cane. Searching for $5,000 they thought was on the premises, the murderers left Novarro's home with $45 in cash. It was a sad and violent end to the often lucky, star-studded life of one of the most revered and adored Latino male leads ever, Ramón Novarro, the very essence of the classic Latin lover.

The versatile Pedro De Córdoba was a character actor of the silent film era. A New Yorker born of Cuban/French parents, Pedro was a tall, gaunt presence of numerous silent films. He had formerly been an opera bass and stage actor. In film he typically portrayed elegant, aristocratic Latinos. He could be quite charming and benevolent, though he was not limited to a sweet demeanor. Often he was cast as the sinister and menacing villain.

In 1911, he was seen in a Mexican version of *Joan of Arc,* and a year later he performed in *Mexican Revolutionists.* More notably, in 1915, Pedro starred in Paramount's *Carmen* as Escamillo, the bullfighter. The film was described as having a flame-like quality.

Geraldine Farrar played Carmen in this five-reel silent shot in 35 mm. The film is still listed as a high achievement for Cecil B. DeMille, who produced and directed the screenplay adapted from a novel by Prosper Mérimée.

"José kills Carmen and then himself while the film cuts over to the triumph of Escamillo in the ring … then Escamillo comes out and stares in horror as José lifts Carmen's head for one kiss and sinks on her body."

In *Temptation*, a Lubin film also released in 1915, De Córdoba worked with Ormi Hawley and a very big snake, as the public viewed with hungry appreciation another delicacy of erotic romance.

De Córdoba also appeared in *María Rosa, Runaway Romany, The New Moon, The World and His Wife, The Inner Chamber, When Knighthood Was in Flower, The Purple Highway, Enemies of Women, The Desert Sheik, The Bandolero, The New Commandment* and *The Crusades*.

De Córdoba was widely known for his many performances of Father Junipero Serra, founder of the California missions. A good Catholic, he married Eleanor Mary Nolan and had six kids.

Don Alvarado, yet another important Latin lover, got his first break in 1924 as an extra in *Mademoiselle Midnight*. Also credited as Don Page, his real name was José Paige. He also became a heartthrob overnight. He did *The Pleasure Buyers* and *Satan in Sables,* both in 1925, and worked in *The Night Cry* and *His Jazz Bride* in 1926. He was at his most sensual in *The Loves of Carmen* with Dolores Del Río.

Above left Don Alvarado.

Above: A rare head shot of Pedro de Córdoba.

He also starred in *The Monkey Talks*, the story of a traveling French circus. The movie featured an undersized man playing a monkey, yet *Photoplay* considered this film, directed by Raoul Walsh, as one of the best of its kind. Other films starring Alvarado include *Captain Thunder*, *Black Beauty* and *Battle of the Sexes*. He was described as "dark and polished, every inch the Spanish Caballero." A native of Albuquerque, New Mexico, he was half Spanish and half English. Though he got his start in silent films, his career would not truly flourish until the talkies.

In his first film, *Fifty-Fifty*, a silent made in 1925, Duncan Renaldo was cast in the story of a wealthy businessman who takes a trip to Paris and falls in love with a woman who is a fashion model by day and a French tango-Apache dancer by night. Renaldo, who never knew his parents or his exact date of birth, arrived in America in the twenties as a stoker on a Brazilian coal ship. His questionable citizenship forced him to live as an outlaw for many years in this country before going on to become one of the biggest Latino luminaries of his time and starring in many films and series, especially Westerns.

And Gilbert Roland, who made his debut as an extra at the tender age of thirteen, was a Latin lover who sizzled with sensuality, rivaling the best of them. But he could also flawlesly step into a role of comedic genius with just as much finesse. He could be a performer of great pride or great humility, whatever the role required. He could be either hot or hilarious! Because of his great versatility, he was known as a virtuoso in the film world. Roland played the gambling dice player Johnny Powell in *The Dove*. The story line had Johnny in love with a dance hall girl, portrayed by Norma Talmadge. Framed for murder, the couple is in front of a firing squad when the gathered crowd cries for freedom on behalf of the lovers. The plot held forth a dream of young love conquering fear and passion. Talmadge said it was one of her most exciting roles. In 1925, Donald Keith and Clara Bow were his partners in *The Plastic Age*, a story about a young student (Roland) whose flirtation with Clara Bow and his inability to resist her bee-stung lips drives him to near madness. Clark Gable can be spotted in this film playing football.

At left: Duncan Renaldo.

Opposite Page: Fernando Lamas and Gilbert Roland, two competing Latino leading men throughout their respective careers.

In *Camille* (1926) Roland went from obscurity to prominence overnight. He was a stunning lover of great passion and pathos in this film. In *The Love Mart*, filmed a year later, Roland is a sexy and colorful romantic. Based on the romance *The Code* of Victor Jallot, penned by Edward Childs Carpenter, the story tells of old New Orleans during slavery. A leisurely, glamorous atmosphere of the Old South permeates the film. In this love drama Roland plays the title character Victor Jallot, who wields a mean rapier and has all the women wild about him. The love of Jallot's life is legally designated as a "lost" octoroon slave. Our hero faces actor Noah Berry, as the dirty villain and must bid for the physical possession of his lover on the auction block.

Roland enjoyed a long and successful career as an actor, and was always a favorite of the audience, no matter the time or place.

In 1926 Paramount teamed up the handsome Roland with Bebe Daniels in *The Campus Flirt*, a sexy romp featuring a lot of girls in athletic attire as members of a female track team. Another Latino favorite of the time, Bebe was of Spanish and Scottish heritage, and also enjoyed a long and impressive career in silent pictures. Though she was impish and warm, an appealing silent comedienne, throughout her body of work in film, she came to embody the essence of the female Latin lover.

Her first screen appearance was in Otis Turner's *The Common Enemy* released in 1910. Daniels also performed in a number of Westerns. She is recorded as having acted in 200 two-reel comedies. She was often billed as the Charming Little Comedienne. In 1919 she worked for the legendary Cecil B. DeMille in *Male and Female*. Thomas Meighan played the lead, while Daniels played a concubine in a Babylon sequence. The next year she did *Why Change Your Wife?* with Gloria Swanson, played the leading lady in Sam Wood's *Dancing Fool* and did a trilogy of comedies with Maurice Campbell in which she played a madcap heiress.

In the DeMille film released in 1921, The *Affairs of Anatol*, Daniels portrays a character named Satan Synne. The same year the actress had a much publicized run-in with the law. Caught speeding by the Los Angeles County Police, the movie screen diva spent ten days in jail.

At Left: Poster art for New York Nights *with Norma Talnmadge and Latino star Gilbert Roland as the male lead.*

Facing page: Neil Hamilton with Bebe Daniels in Paramount Famous Lasky Corp. 1928 film What a Night.

Bebe Daniels performed in a number of Westerns and is recorded as having acted in 200 two-reel comedies often billed as the Charming Little Comedienne.

Though incarcerated, she still received special treatment. Perhaps the police prided themselves on the capture of so brilliant a star. When people came to visit the criminal, the jailer would announce their arrival, to which Ms. Daniels would reply, "Tell them I'm not in."

The publicity didn't hurt much, and the next year she did a film about a movie queen who goes to jail. It was appropriately titled *The Speed Girl*. Increasingly cast as a playgirl opposite Joan Crawford and Gloria Swanson, her repertoire grew tenfold.

In *Unguarded Women* we see a screen rarity, at least for Bebe, when she portrays a woman on a path of destruction. Set in China, the talented Latina plays a World War I widow who leads a reckless, unbridled life. Eventually, she decides that suicide is her only release from the tortures of this world.

In 1923 Daniels worked in another film based on real-life drama. *World's Applause*, produced by Paramount, this time with William DeMille at the helm, was loosely based on the Mary Miles Minter and William Desmond Taylor scandal of 1922. The plot has a woman driven by notoriety and fame, who gets involved in a murder scandal that almost destroys her. In real life, William Desmond Taylor, the director, had been mysteriously murdered. The actress Mary Miles Minter had been linked with him in an intimate relationship, and the scandal ruined her career.

Then she was matched up with Valentino in *Monsieur Beaucaire in 1924*. When asked what she thought of him, Bebe said: "Valentino is the most modest man I ever met in my life." Valentino was wearing a very tight corset by this time, and some cruel reporters wrote that he was developing "jowls."

Above: Poster art for The Son of the Sheik, *staring Rudolph Valentino, the most prominent of all Latin lovers and still adored by countless fans up to this date.*

Bebe Daniels performed as *Miss Bluebeard* in 1925 and played an impressive, fiery "Señorita" in *Volcano* a year later. She became the female equivalent of the Latin lover in films like *She's A Sheik!* in 1927, *Hot News*, opposite Neil Hamilton, and in Gregory La Cava's *Feel My Pulse* and *What a Night!*

Often in risqué situations and photographed in all manner of lace, feathers and jewels, Daniels was a stunning, exotic beauty, as well as an everlasting talent. Married in 1930 to Ben Lyon, the couple became one of cinema's most popular couples, a popularity lasting until her death in 1971.

Ricardo Cortez, here in a heated scene with Greta Garbo, was the most well-known impersonator of the Latin lover — his real name was Jacob Krantz and he was born in Vienna.

Latin lovers were in such demand that people were "impersonating" Latinos. The most well-known impersonator was Ricardo Cortez, whose real name was Jacob Krantz. Having been first a runner on Wall Street and then a stock broker, he made over 350 movies. He started his film career at the age of 35 in *Sixty Cents an Hour* in 1923. Most people didn't know that he was an Austrian Jew, born in Vienna. Those who did know kept it a secret, and he enjoyed a lengthy career as a Latin lover. He did *13 Women* and *Feet of Clay* and was the Spaniard of the title character in *The Spaniard* opposite Alma Rubens. He was billed above Garbo in *The Torrent*, her first film. He was also seen in *Torch Singer*. He once commented that his favorite actresses were Joan Crawford for her tigress ways and Irene Dunne for her spiritual qualities.

Silent films: never heard and now sadly seldom seen. Those that have not disintegrated into dust are likely gathering dust in the corner of some warehouse. Revival houses and film schools seem to be their only contemporary venues, yet viewing these great beginnings of film can constitute an unrivaled luxury: to be witness to the beginnings of an art form, an art form that would impact civilization for all time and experience firsthand the nuances of the silent film era and take a ride atop that first ripple of the ever-expanding wave of cinema.

But soon sound and moving pictures merged to redefine the art form of making movies. And curiously, it was also Edison, that memorable inventor, who was the first to record sound synchronized to a moving film image. That first audible film performance was by Fred Ott, Edison's employer. The significant and worthy event: a sneeze.

Gezundheit! And then, there was sound.

Chapter 3

IT TALKS!....
The little known success of
Hollywood Spanish Language Films

Hollywood silent films were a major success in the international market. They were extremely popular and profitable, especially in the Spanish-speaking world, a growing, entertainment-avid culture just next door to the United States that stretched throughout the entire continent of South America. But that was about to change radically, mostly for the betterment of the art of filmmaking, and for the benefit of moviegoers all around the world.

By 1929, the "all talking! all singing! all dancing!" placards had been up for a couple of years and the profits went sky-high in the domestic market, however all the revenues that the Hollywood studios had been reaping from the lucrative Spanish-speaking market were all of a sudden gone.

The year 1927 gave us the first Academy Awards, designed to honor a growing artistic and creative endeavor and to highlight the importance of a hugely profitable enterprise. That same year the entertainment business saw the emergence of a technical advancement that would change the motion picture industry forever. Warner Brothers produced a film that was to be seen and, more important, heard around the world: *The Jazz Singer*, starring Al Jolson.

Above: Rita Hayworth in a hot screen musical number now possible thanks to the advent of sound on films.

Page 53: The complete cast of The Cat and the Canary (La Voluntad del Muerto), *a film done in both English and Spanish language, pose for a photo on set.*

With this innovation, the audience could enjoy the singing and hear the whole dialogue through the patented Vitaphone process. The still-controversial image of Jolson's painted face and his colorful depiction of a Jewish cantor's son impersonating a Negro jazz performer, kick-started the use of sound in film, establishing new standards and opening the doors to new possibilities and newer and more exciting ventures.

The advent of sound allowed the art of moving pictures to grow and develop in unexpected ways. Movies were now fully embracing the use of words, as spoken by the characters themselves, allowing for stronger dramatic possibilities. Plus, filmmakers could now include music and sound effects. But when movies began to talk, some screen careers were tragically silenced. High-pitched voices or simply the fear of the intimidating and clumsy microphones required by this new technology, put an end to the presence on screen of several early movie personalities. The use of drugs and alcohol, some domestic dramas and a good number of scandals highlighted the demise of a decaying Silent Era royalty who could not cope with the expansive nature of the new medium.

Stage actors with their well-trained voices and stage manners became the vogue. Many of the silent screen stars, Douglas Fairbanks, Dolores Del Río, William Powell, and Ramón Novarro, to name a few, welcomed with ease this novel technology, remaining as popular as they had been before sound made its presence felt.

By 1929, the "all talking! all singing! all dancing!" placards had been up for a couple of years, and profits were sky-high in the domestic market. However, all the revenue that the Hollywood studios had been reaping from the lucrative Spanish-speaking market was suddenly gone.

The movers and shakers of the industry, obviously concerned by this fact, began to brainstorm on what could be done to remain in power in the international arena. The solution hit them with the undeniable logic of a ton of bricks: Use the technology to solve the problem. Why not produce films in Spanish and other languages?

The idea of producing a film in Spanish was first proposed by the then-powerful RKO Pictures. In 1929, the studio produced the musical *Rio Rita*, which became a smash box-office hit in the U.S. So, the studio decided that it was the ideal movie to test

Poster art for the early Blockbuster Rio Rita.

Above: A scene of Rio Rita. *The Spanish version of this movie did so well that it became the motivation to get the wagon rolling and the Spanish versions on screen.*

the waters of a bilingual production. The Spanish version of *Rio Rita* did so well that it became the motivating force to get the wagon rolling and Spanish versions of popular Hollywood hits on screen.

Immediately following RKO's hit, Pathé Studios released *Her Private Affair*, and it, too, met with great success. Looking to reap the benefits of this enormous and movie-hungry market south of the border, Hollywood studios arranged to build polyglot film-producing facilities within their own studio systems. The best Spanish-speaking talent from around the world was hired to make Spanish versions of the most remarkable Hollywood films of the time. The studios also produced films in several other foreign languages (Italian, German and French), however the majority of the films were dubbed into or fully produced in Spanish.

Buster Keaton, the famous comedian, also participated in films done in Spanish.

Hollywood movies produced in Spanish became a big deal, beginning to take strong and definite shape by 1930. Sono Art-World Wide, an aggressive independent company, took a giant step by producing the first American feature film entirely shot in Spanish. Sono copied frame by frame a film that they had already made in English. The Hollywood blockbuster movie *Blaze of Glory* became "Sombras de Gloria" with José Bohr, Mona Rico, Cesar Vanoni, Tito Davidson, and Francisco Morán comprising the cast of this history-making production, all under the direction of Alfred L. Stone.

In all, there were 38 Spanish-language movies produced in Hollywood during 1930. MGM's first venture was the Spanish remake of the musical *Free and Easy*, made the same year under the helm of director Edward Sedgwick. Adapted by Salvador de Alberich and renamed *"Estrellados"*, the film starred one of the finest comedians ever, the unforgettable Buster Keaton, with Raquel Torres as his co-star, and was also directed by Sedgwick.

Estrellados was so successful that after Keaton finished making *Doughboys* in which "he wins the war single-handed, but is shell-shocked by a kiss," the studio did a copy/remake under the title *De Frente, Marchen,* with the very popular star Conchita Montenegro as his love interest. Again, both versions were directed by Sedgwick. This would be a treat for any director: to make two version of the same film in two languages, employing actors of completely opposite backgrounds and cultures. The mood on these sets was electrifying and fast, with some directors working around the clock to make both versions of a movie simultaneously.

Paramount's answer to MGM's success in Spanish-speaking films was an all-star extravaganza titled *"Galas De La Paramount"*, with a trainload of their best and most popular directors: Ernst Lubitsch, Frank Tuttle, Edmund Golding, Dorothy Arzner and a number of others. For their Spanish versions they added performers La Argentina, Rosita Moreno, Ernesto Vilches, Juan Pulido and Ramón Pereda to the original cast. The Spanish and Japanese segments were directed by Eduardo D. Venturini.

As opportunities began to open up, the creative juices of many Latinos began to flow. Hollywood Spanish Pictures Company called upon Xavier Cugat, a young man of many talents, to produce, write and direct *Charros, Gauchos y Manotas*. A young and handsome Luis Alonso, who later on became famous under the screen name Gilbert Roland, made his debut in Spanish films in *Monsieur Le Fox*, directed by Hal Roach.

The Latin community in Hollywood was in high gear. Fox signed Mona Maris to star in *Del Mismo Barrio,* a copy of Victor Fleming's *The Common Clay,* co-starring Juan Torena and René Cardona. Maris, who had one of those long Spanish names often parodied by the screen, Rosa Emma Mona María Marta Capdevielle, was born in Santander, Spain, and moved to California, where she lived most of her life playing supporting roles in a wide variety of movie projects. Universal entered the Spanish-film revolution with *La Voluntad Del Muerto* featuring the popular silent film star Antonio Moreno alongside Lupita Tovar, Conchita Ballesteros, Paul Ellis and María Calvo. While Paramount waited impatiently for Moreno to finish so he could star with Ramón Pereda, María Alba and Barry Norton in *El Cuerpo Del Delito*, another copy of a Hollywood hit, this time Frank Tuttle's *The Benson Murder Case* was being shot.

Another idol of the silver screen, the great Ramón Novarro, got a shot at the Spanish-speaking movie race when he not only starred in MGM's *Sevilla De Mis Amores*, but also directed the film, originally produced as *Call of the Flesh.*

Latin artists were being invited to share their talents among MGM, Universal, Paramount, Warner Brothers, Fox, Columbia, Twentieth Century, CI-TI-GO Studios, and other smaller companies, such

Hollywood Spanish Pictures Company called upon Xavier Cugat to produce, write and direct Charros, Gauchos y Manotas.

as Hollywood Spanish Pictures, First National and Chris Phillis Productions. For Latinos, the word "co-star" was new and exciting, with more magic than it has today. To be any kind of star meant having the universe at your feet, enjoying all the pleasures on earth, avoiding taxes, eating wonderful foods, drinking gin by the gallon, driving fancy motorcars, living in mansions, and basking in plenty of notoriety.

Executives at Paramount were so overwhelmed with their success in the foreign market that they built a studio in Europe so as to make pictures less expensive and to be more conveniently located near their new market. At their facilities in Joinville, France, the studio produced six Spanish films in 1930 and eight in 1931. They signed Cannen Larreleiti and Felix de Pomes to star in most of the films.

During the years 1930 and 1931, the rule of supply and demand was in high gear and saw MGM and Fox joining Paramount in the Spanish market "gold rush."

Film pioneer William Fox, the genius behind Fox Studios, immediately saw the huge potential of the market and gave orders to all his executives to be on the lookout for Latin talent. Unlike all the other major studios, which combined produced a dozen Spanish-language films between 1932 and 1935, Fox kept the sky lit with Spanish stars by producing a total of 41 films over a six-year period.

Hispanic actors, writers and technicians felt lucky to be employed and participating in these films, considering the turmoil and bread lines caused by the Great Depression following the seller's panic on Wall Street in 1929.

The 1930s were a joyous decade for Hispanics in Hollywood. New stars were being discovered, and Spanish-speaking audiences around the world were enjoying the positive images portrayed on the big screen.

> *William Fox saw the huge potential of the market and gave orders to all his executives to be on the look-out for Latin talent. Fox kept the sky lit with Spanish stars by producing a total of forty-one films over a six year period.*

Mona Maris and Carlos Gardel in a scene from Cuesta Abajo, *one of many films produced originally in Spanish in New York by Paramount and featuring Gardel, the famous Argentinian tango singer, their biggest star at the time.*

Lupita Tovar and Antonio Moreno also shared screen credits during this golden era of Hollywood movies made in Español.

The story of the rise of Mona Rico, who had been an extra in pictures before her discovery by director Ernst Lubitsch, is a clichéd one. Yet this slice of real-life rags-to-riches drama is a tale worthy of being told. It seems that Lubitsch was in the process of shooting a screen test with an actor whom he was considering for his next film. The actor was giving his all to the monologue, but something was missing. Lubitsch kept telling the actor to do it one more time, many times.

Finally, Lubitsch turned to the extras standing by, pointed to Mona, called her over, and told her to react to what the actor was saying. Nervously she obeyed. When Lubitsch saw the rushes, he forgot about the actor he had been having so much trouble with and concentrated on the surprising small performance by the beautiful extra. He sent out a posse of underlings to search for the sexy unknown. The dream of millions of young women came true for her: She went from a $7.50-a-day extra to John Barrymore's co-star.

A number of stars such as Ramón Novarro, Lupe Veléz, Dolores Del Río and Antonio Moreno were constantly working, since they were in demand to make films in both languages. Del Río received superstar treatment in her first RKO picture, which was appropriately titled *Girl of the Rio,* opposite Leo Carrillo, who played a Mexican caballero. RKO's next vehicle for Del Río was a film that is still a classic today, *Flying Down to Rio* in which she and Gene Raymond receive top billing, co-starring with Raul Roulien. The film's captivating "Carioca" number was nominated for an Academy Award and, as a result, two new stars emerged: Fred Astaire and Ginger Rogers, RKO's class act for many years to come.

The use of this new technology provided for the creation of some amazing and long-lasting Hollywood hits. Sound and image came together and contributed to the growth of an art form. And the Latinos were always present, contributing with their very own sound... but En Español.

Chapter 4

ALLÁ EN EL RANCHO GRANDE!....
The era of the "Shoot-em-ups"

A film is only as good as its villain is bad! From The Alamo to Zorro, Latino talent permeated the Western genre from A to Z. Often depicted as the bad guy, the unjust portrayal of the Latino as an impervious villain has been well documented and rightfully acknowledged by several recent publications and historical accounts, making it, understandably, the subject of much debate and furor. In this writing we take the time to salute those unforgettable Hispanic cowboy heroes and villains. And, oh yes!, what likeable heroes they were, and how convincing the villains they played!

Although Edison was the father of the one-reel drama, the very first "real" movie ever made, one featuring a creative approach to the new media, implementing the element of film editing for dramatic effects, and actually telling a full story, was the pioneering Western *The Great Train Robbery* (1903). This short film (long for its time at approximately nine minutes) directed by Edwin S. Porter, later named 'the father of the story film,' marked a milestone in movie-making for its storyboarding of the script, first use of title cards, an ellipsis, a panning shot, and cross-cutting editing techniques.

While ground breaking "shoot-em-up" fare, this was not by all accounts the first Western ever. However, it features a stunning close-up (the first in cinema's history) of gunman Justus D. Barnes firing directly into the camera... and into the audience. The most commercially successful film of the pre-nickelodeon era, the scene was described at the time as unsettling. This shocking sequence was later paid homage to by director Martin Scorsese in his modern gangster masterpiece, *Goodfellas*.

Las Norias Bandit Raid: A day that will live in infamy! Texas Rangers with dead bandidos, October 8, 1915.

The Greaser

Cowboys and gunslingers played prominent roles in Westerns, often battling it out with Native Americans and other lowlifes, cutthroats and crooked types. Early Westerns frequently portrayed "Injuns" and Mexicans or "greasers" (who were generally perceived by the public as any character of Latino origin hailing from either Spain, Argentina, Cuba or even Brazil - more on this later) as dishonorable villains, slithering and conniving bad guys.

Fast on the heels of the mythic Latin lover, so popular during the first attempts at onscreen drama and romance comes the negative depiction of Latinos viewed through the film-lens, a perspective perpetuating on the silver screen one of history's most infamous racial slurs to date: The Greaser. The Latino Hollywood community has come a long way by battling it out with the poncho-wearing, burro-riding, knife-wielding, gun-toting, lazy sombrero-over-the-face, siesta-sleeping, tequila-drinking and señorita-chasing stereotype portrayed by most early films, specifically Westerns.

"Most Americans distrust our southern neighbors, on account of they're darker and shorter. They are viewed as a race apart, as well as a past foe."

William S. Hart

At right: An early 20th Century Mexican worker, a far cry from the bandido made famous by the big screen.

Facing page: William S. Hart, a Shakespearian stage actor, became a celebrity of Westerns in the silent film era, writing, directing, and acting in them.

The strongest reason for this negative depiction of Hispanics, according to George Hadley-García's book *Hispanic Hollywood: The Latins in Motion Pictures*, was blatant racism. Hadley-García quotes William S. Hart as saying during the 1920s, "Most Americans distrust our southern neighbors, on account of they're darker and shorter. They are viewed as a race apart, as well as a past foe."

The book also places most of the blame for the negative depiction of the "Mexican," the racist classification of all other Hispanics under the slur of oily "greaser," even the at-first-glance benign portrayal of the silly "bandido," on the broad shoulders of the Western genre. That, following some undeniable logic and a very specific reason, at the time "films set in urban America never include Hispanics, and Western stories set in Latin America were not-existent." Actors or actresses sporting a skin complexion with a sprinkle of cinnamon, a hint of olive or even the exoticism of milk and chocolate were boxed into the roles of servants, lowly villains or anonymous henchmen by the Hollywood movie-making machine. During this time female Latino characters were not even allowed to kiss their Anglo counterparts on screen, a far cry from today's Jennifer López getting top billing and kissing the guy (and getting to keep him to boot) in modern romantic comedies.

Mexicans, and for some strange reason all Latinos, were viewed by North Americans as traditional foes during the late 19th century as well as the early 1920s. The year 1898 brought with it the Spanish American War, which followed a 50 year period in which the United States saw the hardships of the Mexican-American War (1846–1848), the annexation of Texas and California, and the ensuing sense of competition among Americans and their neighbors south of the border. To top it all off, in 1918 a virulent disease broke out, infamously named the Spanish influenza, a mysterious ailment which spread throughout the land killing more people than the recently concluded World War I. So the common folk resisted and even resented everything and everyone Latin.

The 'Greaser' characterization not only vilified, but ridiculed Hispanics. Usually an incompetent, idiotic, sadistic and ruthless villain, whose vices and deviant behavior outdid all other "paler villains" put together.

The word "greaser," a derogatory term in the 19th century for any Mexican living in what is now the southwest United States, is believed to be derived from one of the lowliest occupations typically held by Mexicans laborers at the time, the greasing of the axles of mule carts. Some scholars suggest the term comes from the practice by those very same laborers, most of them of Indian or Mexican descent, of greasing their backs to facilitate the unloading of hides and cargo, while others suggest it is rooted in a perceived similarity between Mexican skin color and grease.

The term was actually incorporated into an early California statute, the Greaser Act of 1855, a dubious piece of legislation shamelessly disguised as an anti-vagrancy statute. The law defined a vagrant as "all persons who are commonly known as 'Greasers' or the issue of Spanish and Indian blood… and who go armed and are not peaceable and quiet persons." This act of law was an expression of a virulent form of anti-Mexican sentiment among many Anglo Californians and was repealed a few years later

But the origin of the term may even be more offensive still; the "greaser" label may derive from the long-standing misconception of Mexicans as unkempt and unclean, sporting unwashed, "greasy" black hair. While the term originated as a derogatory reference toward those of Mexican origin, its use expanded over time to encompass Peruvian and Chilean miners during the California gold rush and, more broadly, to describe anyone of Spanish origin. Its original usage appears to have also been sexualized, used as a way of describing a "treacherous Mexican male who was sexually threatening to and desirous of white women."

Facing page: Pancho Villa, considered by the United States a Mexican bandit leader, seen here in a photo circa 1916, is regarded as a nationalist hero among many Hispanics.

Hollywood embraced this label to describe its unflattering creation of despicable Mexicans, frontier "bandidos" capable of theft and all other kinds of mischief, even rape and murder. Familiar enough, the term adorned the marquee with titles like *The Greaser's Gauntlet*, *Tony the Greaser*, *The Girl and the Greaser*, *The Greaser's Revenge*, *Bronco Billy and the Greaser*, and, simply, *The Greaser*.

Although uniformly evil and deceiving, the "greaser" character created by Hollywood during the beginning of the 20th century occasionally had a good heart. The movie advertisement for the silent film *Tony the Greaser* is a good example of the force carried by the stereotype of the enemy "greaser" and its common use for referring to all those of Mexican descent: "From force of habit, some might call him a 'Greaser'; true, he is a Mexicano, but a man of noble instincts and chivalrous nature."

The "greaser" characterization not only vilified but also ridiculed Hispanics. Usually an incompetent, idiotic, sadistic and ruthless villain, whose vices and deviant behavior outdid all other "paler villains" put together, this damaging figure paraded itself across a wide spread of early Western adventures. And the Hispanic did fight back. In response to this negative depiction of Hispanics by the movie medium in Hollywood, the Mexican government issued a formal protest in 1919, and by the year 1922 it banned all movies that gave unfair and negative portrayal of Latinos.

During the 1930s a slew of Latin American countries, with Mexico at the forefront, issued a threat to pull out from purchasing any films featuring such negative Latino types. The fear of losing distribution of Hollywood films to some very important Mexican and Latin American markets urged the Production Code Administration (Hollywood's self-policing body at the time) to help eliminate the most virulent anti-Hispanic references from films made by Hollywood studios, especially all references to the "greaser."

Latino Cowboys and Cowgirls

Latinos, nonetheless, have been a strongly felt presence in Westerns since the early inception of this genre into the movie-making pantheon. Stars like Antonio Moreno, Gilbert Roland, Dolores Del Río and José Crespo, all of them first-rate Latino Hollywood artists with an ample list of silent-era movie credits, were billed in some early Western classics. But these names, with all their fame and undeniable prominence in the

Hollywood constellation of stars, are only the tip of the proverbial iceberg. Names of Hispanic performers have been present on movie credits since the very beginnings of the film era, the Western genre being no exception.

The list is extensive and spans decades of filmmaking. Actress Rita Hayworth, at the time billed with her real name of Rita Cansino, started her relationship with the art of moving pictures in several classic Westerns. Even famed Mexican "revolucionario" Pancho Villa was himself the subject, and even the star, of an early screen treatment. The bold, daring and utterly romantic bandolier-wearing warrior from south of the border, a very peculiar character as well as an important Mexican historic figure, signed an agreement to allow a Hollywood crew to follow him around and keep track of traumatic wartime events, closely tracking most of his battles and military movements and documenting all on film. This attempt constitutes a pioneering step toward dramatic "unscripted reality" filmmaking, but one which proved to be quite a difficult task for all those involved. The affair required that attacks and other sensitive military exercises be postponed until the cameras were in place, obviously losing in the process it's 'cinema verité' quality as well as all strategic or military value. Villa's life was later fictionalized several times and treated for the movie screen, with Spanish actor Antonio Banderas playing his latest incarnation.

The *Mexican Spitfire*, Lupe Vélez, was a regular early-days cowboy counterpart. Even the sensuous Raquel Torres, who had a brief stint in Hollywood after the advent of sound, appears in *The Desert Rider* a standard Western of the era. According to scholars, she "provided spicy set decoration" opposite cowboy star Tim McCoy. Modern viewers can still get a sampling of her doings on screen in *Duck Soup*, one of the Marx Brothers' comedy films. It was Raquel who inspired Groucho's classic line: "I could dance with you until the cows came home. On second thought, I'd rather dance with the cows until you came home." Born Paula Osterman in Hermosillo, Mexico, she arrived in films at the age of 19 and garnered instant attention and a flurry of wolf whistles in W.S. Van Dyke's *White Shadows in the South Seas*. Best known as MGM's first movie to synchronize music, dialogue and sound effects, this is the film supposedly in which the MGM lion roared before the opening credits for the first time.

Actresses like Mona Maris, featured as a supporting actress on many films, started her prolific screen career during the Silent Era and was featured in many now-classic Westerns. Another name commonly found on some of those early attempts at Westerns was Soledad Jiménez, who made a career as a supporting actress in many films. Starting as early as 1929, when her credit appears in the film *In Old Arizona*, directed by Raoul Walsh and starring one of history's most renowned cowboys, Warner Baxter, the actress was often credited on films as Solidad Jimines, Soledad Jiminez and Solidad Jimenez.

Facing Page: The perfect Mexican bandido, Alfonso Bedoya was a Mexican character actor who achieved his greatest success in U.S. films.

"Badges? We ain't got no badges! We don't need no badges. I don't have to show you any stinkin' badges!"

Alfonso Bedoya
as Gold Hat in Treasure of the Sierra Madre

The perfect Mexican bandido, with his weather-beaten face, bushy mustache and menacing, sardonic smile, Alfonso Bedoya was a Mexican character actor who achieved his greatest success in U.S. films. Born in Vicam, Sonora, Mexico, in 1904, he had a nomadic upbringing. As a teen he moved to Houston, Texas, where he attended a private school, but he soon quit and set out working odd jobs to make a living. Eventually he ended up back in Mexico City, where he found work in the Mexican Film Industry. Discovered by Hollywood, he was cast in 1948 as Gold Hat the bandit in *Treasure of the Sierra Madre*, his American film debut with the famous Humphrey Bogart.

His thick Mexican accent put the infamous line: "Badges? We ain't got no badges! We don't need no badges. I don't have to show you any stinkin' badges!" on the map. Bedoya's casual line of dialogue became as classic as the film itself. He made other American films but none to match this film's classic stature. Unfortunately, a problem with alcohol ruined his health and ended his career. He died in Mexico City, on December 15, 1957.

Important Hispanic players in the movie-making business, along many other early screen laborers, laid the groundwork for the rich treasure throve of Latino-rooted screen credits to come.

While Alfonso Bedoya was the perfect bandido, Ysabel Ponciana Paiz played the opposite and more comic Mexican character. Widely known in Hollywood and credited as Chrispin Martin, he was also billed in his films by many other names, such as Chris-Pin Martin, Chris King Martin, Chris Martin, Cris-Pin Martin and Ethier Crispin Martini. He always played the roles of the rotund, bumbling, slow character of Mexican heritage, and also sported a heavy accent when delivering his lines in broken English. With over 100 films between 1925 and 1953, including over 50 Westerns, he is best remembered as sidekick Gordito and Pancho in nine of the *Cisco Kid* films.

Romualdo Tirado, often credited on screen as Romaldo Tirado, had an extensive filmography as actor, writer, director, cinematographer, producer and editor. Born in Quintanar de la Orden, Toledo, Castilla-La Mancha, Spain, from 1910 well into the forties he was credited as an actor in more than 30 films, most of them Westerns.

Supporting actors like Enrique Acosta, Rosita Moreno, Inés Gómez, Julián Rivero, Frank Mayo, Lupita Tovar, Fernando Galvez, Conchita Montenegro, George Regas, Joe de la Cruz, Luis Alberni, Alan García, Joe Domínguez, Steve Clemente, Don Alvarado, Artie Ortego (Art Ardigan) and important players in the movie-making business like movie star Emilio (El Indio) Fernández, Pedro de Córdova, along many other early screen laborers, laid the groundwork for the rich treasure throve of Latino-rooted screen credits to come.

At left: Crispín Martin in character.

Facing page at right: Katy Jurado on the set of High Noon.

Top right: Katy Jurado during the filming of Broken Lance.

It was not until 1954 that a Latino talent was officially recognized by the Hollywood filmmaking community. A Western version of King Lear, Edward Dmytryk's *Broken Lance*, which in 1955 won a best writing Academy Award, featured an exotic beauty hailing from a wealthy family in Guadalajara, Mexico. Katy Jurado played opposite Spencer Tracy, and her portrayal of his Indian wife won her an Academy Award nomination as best supporting actress, making her the first Mexican actress thus honored.

Born María Christina Jurado García, she lived a pampered lifestyle during her early years, but her family's lands were confiscated by the Mexican federal government for redistribution to the landless peasantry. Jurado was just 16 when movie star and filmmaker Emilio Fernandez discovered her and immediately wanted to cast her in his films, but her grandmother objected to her wish to become a movie actress. Jurado eventually made her screen debut in *No matarás* during the Golden Age of Mexican cinema. Her most memorable role in Mexican movies was in *Nosotros los pobres* (*We the Poor*) opposite Mexican cinema's superstar Pedro Infante. Blessed

Katy Jurado and her one-time husband, and also Hollywood star, Ernest Borgnine.

with stunning beauty and an assertive personality, Jurado played strong and determined females in a wide variety of films in Mexico and the United States.

Also a bullfight critic, it was at a *corrida* that Jurado was spotted by John Wayne and director Budd Boetticher (also a professional bullfighter), who cast Jurado in his autobiographical film *Bullfighter and the Lady*, shot in Mexico. Jurado made her big breakthrough in American films in the role of Gary Cooper's former mistress in *High Noon*. The actress remained in Los Angeles, and in 1959 she married Ernest Borgnine, her co-star in *The Badlanders*. Described as a "tempestuous relationship," Jurado and Borgnine separated in 1961, and media outlets reported at the time that Borgnine was abusive. After a rough divorce where they fought over alimony, their separation became final in 1964. After an attempted suicide in 1968, she moved back home to Mexico permanently, though she continued to appear in American films as a character actress.

Her impressive career included work with master Spanish cineaste Luis Buñuel, who cast Jurado in his award-winning Mexican melodrama *El Bruto*. She played sheriff Slim Pickens's wife and partner in Sam Peckinpah's *Pat Garrett and Billy the Kid* and played the wife of Marlon Brando's nemesis Dad Longworth (Karl Malden) in *One-Eyed Jacks*, Brando's sole directorial effort. She appeared on the Western-themed American TV shows *Death Valley Days*, *The Rifleman*, *The Westerner*, and *The Virginian*. Her last appearance in an American film was in Stephen Frears's *The Hi-Lo Country*.

In 1956 Jurado appeared on screen in *Man from Del Rio* with a fellow Mexican national and a popular Latino star: Anthony Quinn. Described as one-quarter Irish, his real name was Anthony Rudolph Oaxaca Quinn, and he hailed from Chihuahua, Mexico, and, unlike Jurado, had become an American citizen. The grandson of a movie-fan granny, who loved the films of Antonio Moreno and Ramón Novarro, she made him "promise to get in movies." The talented Quinn, with features he described as "Aztec," went on to play a diverse number of characters in his long trajectory as a movie star. From Attila the Hun to an Eskimo native, Quinn portrayed Chinese, Rumanians, Greeks, American Indians and, of course, Latino characters. He played opposite Marlon Brando in *Viva Zapata!*. The film, scripted by John Steinbeck and directed by Elia Kazan, tells about the real-life story of Emiliano Zapata, a *campesino* who becomes a hero of the revolution and President of Mexico. Marlon Brando played the famed *revolucionario* and Quinn was cast as his brother Eufemio, garnering his first nomination to an Academy Award for best supporting actor. He also starred in the Western action movie *Guns for San Sebastian* playing Mexican outlaw patriot Leon Alastray, and even worked under the direction of master cineaste Ferderico Fellini in his classic film *La Strada*.

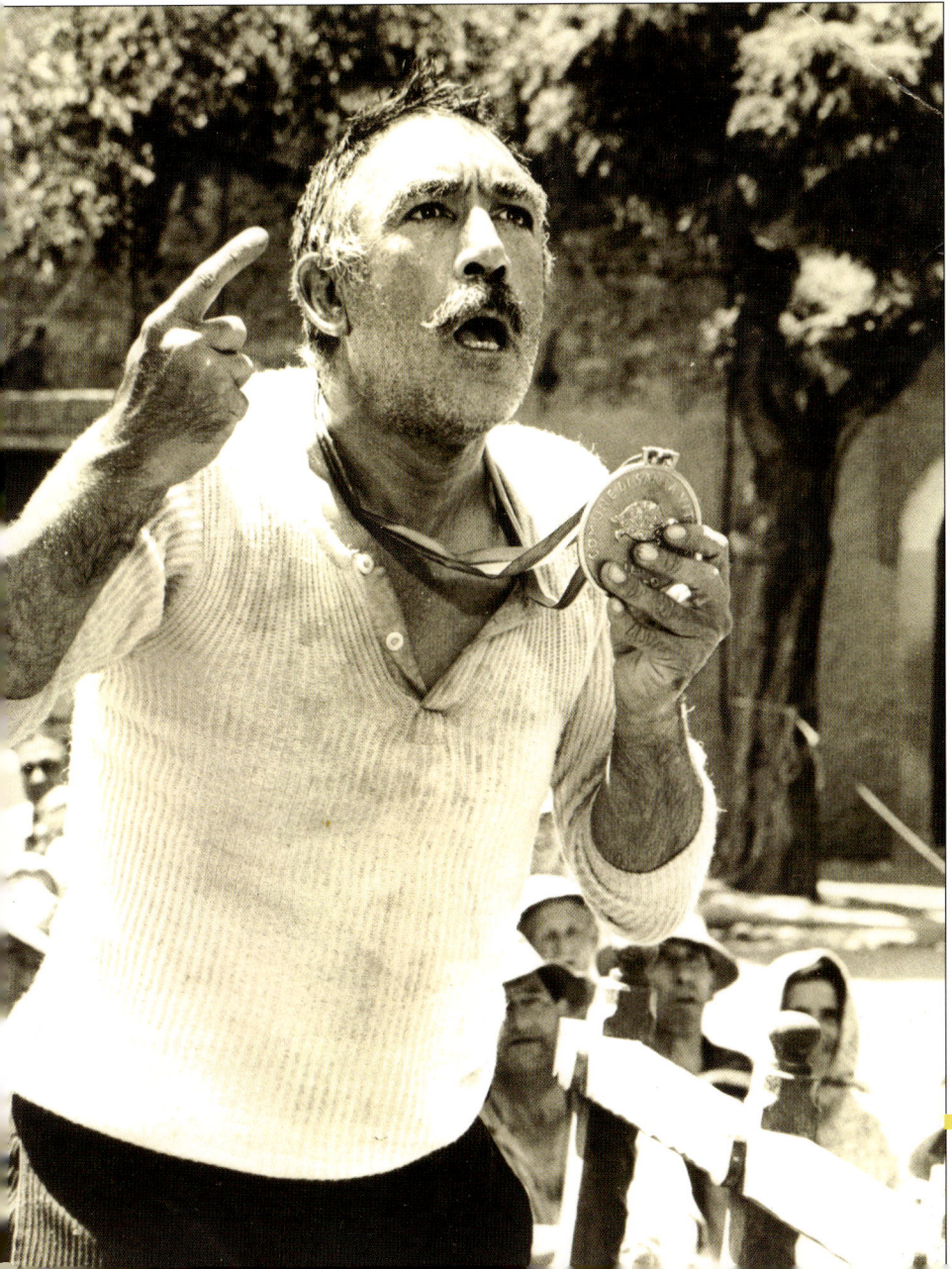

The dialoge in a Western even borrows a lot of Spanish words to enrich and give color to its screen depiction of frontier life and liven up its hero's utterances.

The Western genre itself owes a lot to Hispanic culture. Hispanic Vaqueros roamed the early America as triumphant *conquistadores* on horseback filling the natives with awe, making them the very first cowboys in history. The dialogue in a Western even borrows a lot of Spanish words to enrich and give color to its screen depiction of frontier life and liven up its hero's utterances. Words like *desperado, mano a mano, adios* and the most famous cowboy reference ever coined for the screen: the mythical, lonesome and mysterious *hombre*, are all Spanish words or words rooted in that language.

It is also important to highlight the fact that some Hispanic characters became regular, lasting and most of all, well-beloved heroes of Westerns. Nowadays there are two truly time-defying and all-appealing cowboy heroes, characters that define and set the standard for most all other modern-day superheroes, and they are both Hispanic. The Cisco Kid and El Zorro are two cowboy heroes worthy of praise and detailed consideration. Almost as old as the Western genre itself, and just as resilient, both of these classic cowboy heroes have been the subject of stories and song, novels, book serials and comic books, even radio shows and, most important, they both have been generously treated with numerous screen versions throughout history, even as recently as our 21st century.

Hailing from Chihuahua and with features he described as "Aztec," Anthony Quinn went on to play a diverse number of characters in his long trajectory as a movie star.

The Cisco Kid

Beginning, obviously, in the Silent Era *The Cisco Kid* was translated into film as early as 1914 when William R. Dunn starred in the first movie version of the famous hero in *The Caballero's Way*. Five years later, in 1919, *The Border Terror*, another action adventure Western featuring the Mexican caballero, was made for the silver screen.

The character of the Cisco Kid was actually created by William Sydney Porter under his famous pen name O. Henry. In this short story, ironically titled "A Caballero's Way" and published in 1907, the Kid is not even Hispanic. An Anglo outlaw who has killed six white men and countless Mexicans throughout his criminal life, the Kid described in O. Henry's tale has nothing in common with the clean and romanticized Hollywood treatment. Some screen versions of the Kid don't even have the hero kill the bad guys, tricking them to kill each other instead.

In 1929 Warner Baxter won an Oscar for his portrayal of the Kid in Fox-Movietone's *In Old Arizona*. Noted as the first sound Western produced by a major studio, this was also the film during which the codirector Raoul Walsh, who became an important director of Westerns later in his career, lost an eye.

From then on until 1950, the character was also portrayed by some immortal Latino stars. Actors of the stature of César Romero, Gilbert Roland, who made six Cisco Kid films during 1946 and 1947, and the most famous and recognizable Cisco Kid of them all, Duncan Renaldo, were cast to play the hero. One of the first TV series filmed in color, the aptly titled *The Cisco Kid* featured Renaldo as the heroic Cisco, while Leo Carrillo played his sidekick Pancho. Diablo and Loco were the names of their equally famous horses. A very popular show at the time, 156 episodes were made, and the series ran from 1950 until 1956. *The Cisco Kid* helped Renaldo become a permanent icon in contemporary Western lore.

In 1994 a TV movie was made of the Kid starring the actor of Puerto Rican descent Jimmy Smits as the Kid, proof of the timeless nature of this colorful and beloved Hispanic hero.

Above: Poster art for an early film version of "The Cisco Kid."

Facing Page: The most popular of all Ciscos: Duncan Renaldo.

El Zorro

Another important and fascinating Latino cowboy hero is the dashing Zorro. The mask, the sombrero, the daring feats and risky gymnastics, the light-speed swordplay, and most important, the mark of zorro -the famous Z drawn with three precise slashes of the sword's tip- are now part of our collective cultural inventory.

Zorro (the hero's name sometimes sports the definite article: El Zorro), is the Spanish word for "fox" and is also the name of a character created in 1919 by Johnston McCulley, a pulp fiction writer. The secret identity of Don Diego de la Vega (originally Don Diego Vega), a fictional nobleman and master swordsman living in Spanish-era California, Zorro defends, Robin Hood-style, the poor Mexican farmers and the helpless native serfs from the tyranny and corruption of the evil Spanish governor. *El Zorro* made his first appearance in the serial *The Curse of Capistrano*, McCulley's five-part series published in the pulp magazine *All-Story Weekly*.

Similar to some real bandits in California history, Zorro is often associated with Joaquín Murrieta, better known as the "Mexican Robin Hood." Murrieta's life was fictionalized in an 1854 book by John Rollin Ridge. In 1998 the film *The Mask of Zorro*, starring Antonio Banderas, has Murrieta's brother succeed de la Vega as Zorro. A legendary California robber and delinquent, Murrieta is the main character in several early Westerns. *Robin Hood of El Dorado*, starring Warner Baxter, was the first incursion of the famous and romantic character into film. The character was later exploited in other Westerns like *The Avenger* with Buck Jones and *Old Sacramento*, a B Western featuring the work of William Elliott.

Robin Hood himself is often cited as another possible inspiration, as well as other famed California bandits like Salomón Pico and Tiburcio Vásquez. William Lamport, an Irish soldier living in Mexico in the 17th century whose life was fictionalized by Vicente Riva Palacio in the 19th century, is also mentioned as a possible source for the fictional hero. And, according to many Californians, Estanislao, a Yokuts Indian who led a revolt against the San José Mission in 1827, is actually the real Zorro. Some suggest McCulley drew inspiration from several different sources, including the 1905 novel *The Scarlet Pimpernel*, which features a number of parallels to McCulley's creation. Zorro has been noted as one of the original inspirations for the creation of *The Phantom* and *Batman*, as well as many other comic-strip action heroes.

Douglas Fairbanks and Mary Pickford on their honeymoon selected *The Curse of Capistrano* to become the inaugural picture for their new studio, United Artists. This was to start what would become a cinematic tradition. The success of that silent film, led United Artists to make *The Mark of Zorro*, starring Fairbanks himself as the daring hero, then prompted a 1925 sequel titled *Don Q, Son of Zorro*, featuring Fairbanks once again as Don Diego's grown-up son, Don César, as well as reprising his role as Don Diego.

The character has been featured in a great number of other film versions. *The Bold Caballero* in 1936 starred Robert Livingstone, and *Zorro Rides Again* was released a year later with John Carroll as a modern-day descendent, Jim Vega. *Zorro's Fighting Legion*, a 1939 film project with Reed Hadley as Zorro was followed a year later with another version of *The Mark of Zorro*, this time starring the famous Tyrone Power. In 1944 Linda Stirling played an 1880s female descendent of de la Vega in *Zorro's Black Whip*, followed in 1947 by *Son of Zorro* with George Turner and *Ghost of Zorro* with Clayton Moore, released in 1949. In 1958 actor Guy Williams starred in *Zorro, the Avenger* and *The Sign of Zorro*. Williams also gave life to the masked hero in a Walt Disney-produced television anthology series running from 1957 to 1959.

In 1958 actor Guy Williams stared in the screen versions "Zorro, the Avenger" and "The Sign of Zorro." he also gave life to the masked hero in a Walt Disney-produced television anthology series running from 1957 to 1959.

The Erotic Adventures of Zorro completed in 1972 featured Douglas Fey as Zorro, and in 1974 Mexican actor Pedro Armendáriz, Jr. played the villain in *La Gran Aventura del Zorro.* The film, set in a very primitive San Francisco Bay Area, idealized the Guy Williams portrayal of the character.

Also in 1974, Frank Langella starred in a new version of *The Mark of Zorro,* and in 1975 Zorro met the spaghetti Western, when French actor Alain Delon played Don Diego in his fight with the corrupt Colonel Huerta.

In the 1981 comedic version of the adventure, *Zorro, The Gay Blade*, a parody take on the dashing swordsman starring tan master George Hamilton, our favorite hero breaks his leg just before he is to set out on an adventure and sends his gay twin brother, an expert with the whip, in his stead.

Another version of *The Mask of Zorro* released in 1998, features an anti-Zorro played against tradition. Anthony Hopkins is de la Vega and Antonio Banderas (the first Latino Zorro ever) plays Alejandro Murrieta, a Latino misfit roaming

Previous page: Guy Williams poses for the still camera as El Zorro.

At top: Charles Christian Nahl's earliest image of a Joaquín Murrieta, Mountain Bandit

At right: Another early image of the famous Mexican bandit.

Next page: In the year 2005, Chilean author Isabel Allende published the novel "El Zorro," in which she gives a full fictionalized biography of Diego De la Vega.

In 1998, Antonio Banderas (the first Latino Zorro ever) plays Alejandro Murrieta, a Latino misfit roaming the California landscape and the brother of outlaw Joaquín Murieta, who is groomed to become the next Zorro.

---

the California landscape and the brother of outlaw Joaquín Murrieta, who is groomed to become the next Zorro. This was followed in 2005 with *The Legend of Zorro*, also with Banderas as the latest incarnation of the hero.

Also in the year 2005, Chilean author Isabel Allende published the novel *El Zorro*, in which she gives a fully fictionalized biography of de la Vega and his secret goings-on as the masked hero battling evil along the California coast

As noted earlier, the legend of Zorro is credited with being one of the earliest precursors of the superhero of American comic books. An independently wealthy individual with a secret identity, which he conceals under a disguise, while accomplishing good for the people with his superior fighting abilities and resourcefulness, Zorro laid the foundation for many modern-day super heroes.

Appearing in many different comic book series over the decades, the most revered version was drawn by Alex Toth starting in 1949 and appearing through the 1950s, published by Dell Comics in *Four Color* magazine. After 1968, the Zorro character remained dormant for 20 years, only to be revived by Marvel in 1990 for a 12-issue tie-in with a television series that ran from 1989 to 1993 and starred Duncan Regehr as Zorro. Other comic versions include titles like the outlandish Topps Comics mini-series *Dracula Versus Zorro*, published in 1993.

In addition to features and movie film shorts, comics, TV series, even several animated series, newspaper daily and Sunday strips were also published during the 1990s. Today, the latest comic book version of the adventures of Zorro is drawn in the now-popular Japanese illustration style known as manga. The character has also appeared in several European comics and is universally beloved in Latin America, usually in licensed, translated reprints of American comics.

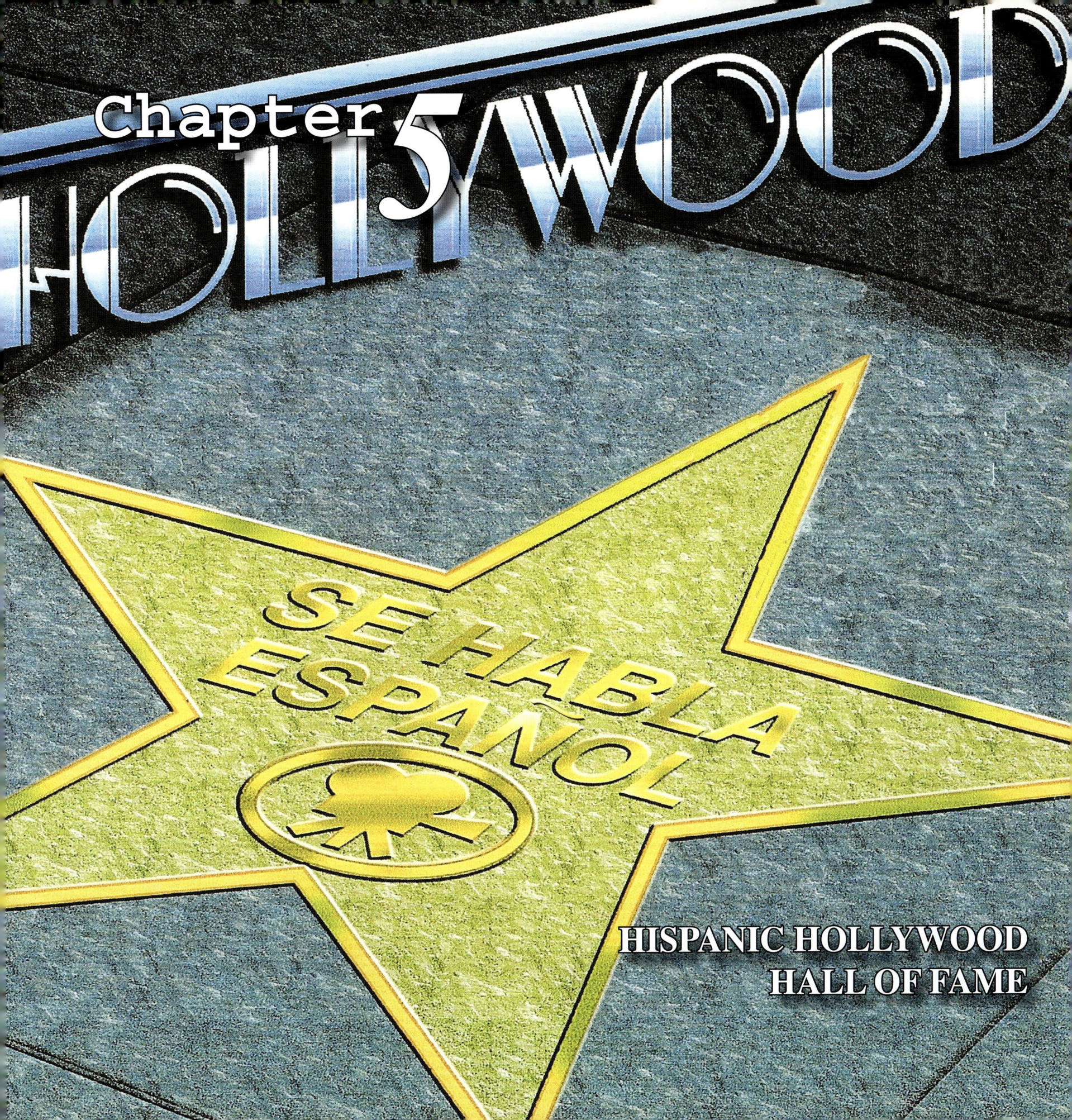

Their contributions deserve more than to be silently pondered, candidly shared and then laid to rest with the remainder of the memories.

These are the faces we recognize, admire and fantasize about. Indelible images of yore, reminding us that the art of the moving image has come a long way in its century-old lifetime. The black and white films, the yellowish patina of the promotional portraits, the anachronistic settings, attires and attitudes —they are all there, still beating strong, waiting to be rediscovered and deserving of being celebrated, cherished and treasured.

More than just some shooting stars crossing the Hollywood sky leaving behind the sweet memories of their fleeting presence, wrapped in the glitter of their volatile galactic dust, these figures aren't just merely the illusion of movement brought upon by the magic of celluloid frames speeding parsimoniously through the projector's mechanism. They are more than the stain of fading light dying over the canvas after the credits roll.

They are human, with human needs and wants, and the protagonists of much more drama than the ones devised by the script and illustrated by the unflinching eye of the camera. They created by their actions a landscape of fantasy, love, thrills and adventure. They sold dreams for the price of an admission ticket and graciously accepted the praise and fame this

The black and white films, the yellowish patina of the promotional portraits, the anachronistic settings, attires and attitudes —they are all there, still beating strong, waiting to be rediscovered and deserving of being celebrated, cherished and treasured.

endeavor demanded in return. They are worthy of praise, not for who they are or what they signify, but for what they gave. Their very essence is trapped within those minute 35 mm frames, quickly unspooling 24 of them every single second, telling of life, love, hope and virtues. They made us laugh and cry, ponder and imagine, dream and live, what more could we ask for?

They placed some noticeable landmarks over the wide map of the movie making world, and we collect all of them here so that we don't forget they did have lives besides the ones displayed on the screen.

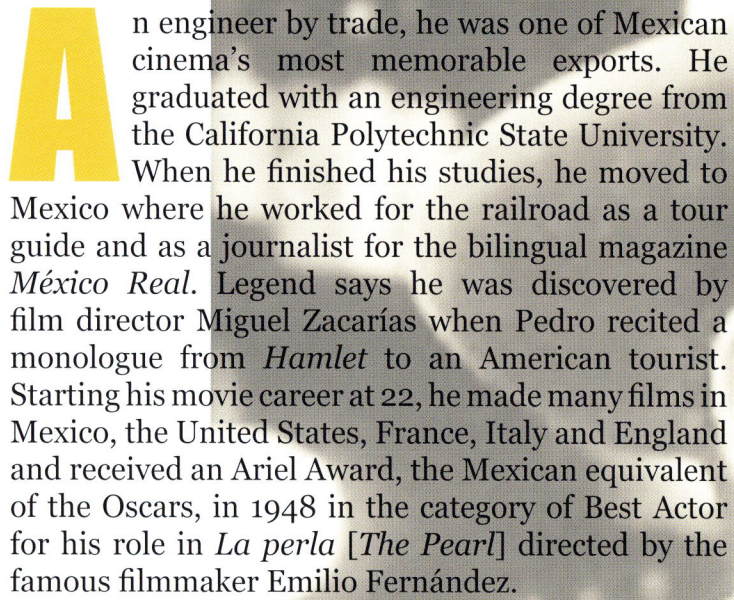

An engineer by trade, he was one of Mexican cinema's most memorable exports. He graduated with an engineering degree from the California Polytechnic State University. When he finished his studies, he moved to Mexico where he worked for the railroad as a tour guide and as a journalist for the bilingual magazine *México Real*. Legend says he was discovered by film director Miguel Zacarías when Pedro recited a monologue from *Hamlet* to an American tourist. Starting his movie career at 22, he made many films in Mexico, the United States, France, Italy and England and received an Ariel Award, the Mexican equivalent of the Oscars, in 1948 in the category of Best Actor for his role in *La perla* [*The Pearl*] directed by the famous filmmaker Emilio Fernández.

**Pedro Armendáriz /
Pedro Gregorio Armendáriz Hastings**
1912 — 1963

Mexico

"You cannot show a pregnant woman on television," the CBS network once told him, back in the time when you could not even use the word "pregnant" on television. But Desi Arnaz did. And his real-life wife, the then very pregnant Lucille Ball, appeared on screen in that very condition. Yet instead of pregnant, the character was only "expecting," according to the heavy accented statement by Ricky Ricardo, the character played by Arnaz. He was born in Santiago de Cuba to a wealthy family (in fact his ancestors had been among the recipients of the original Spanish land grants in the 18th century). During the 1933 Cuban revolution led by Fulgencio Batista, who overthrew the American-backed President Gerardo Machado, the family was stripped of its wealth, property and power, and Arnaz and his parents fled to Florida. A disciple of his mentor, famed orchestra leader Xavier Cugat, he began his career as a professional musician in 1936. His signature song "Babalú" written by Margarita Lecuona (the cousin of famed Cuban composers Ernesto and Ernestina Lecuona), was a big hit of the time, and he introduced American audiences to the "Conga Line," which became a national rage. Arnaz is also credited with the innovation of the multi-camera television system and the invention of the rerun. In addition to *I Love Lucy*, he produced *December Bride*, *The Mothers-in-Law*, *The Lucy Show*, *Those Whiting Girls*, *Our Miss Brooks*, and *The Untouchables*, all of them Top Ten hit shows.

**Desi Arnaz /
Desiderio Alberto Arnaz y de Acha III**
1917 – 1986

Cuba

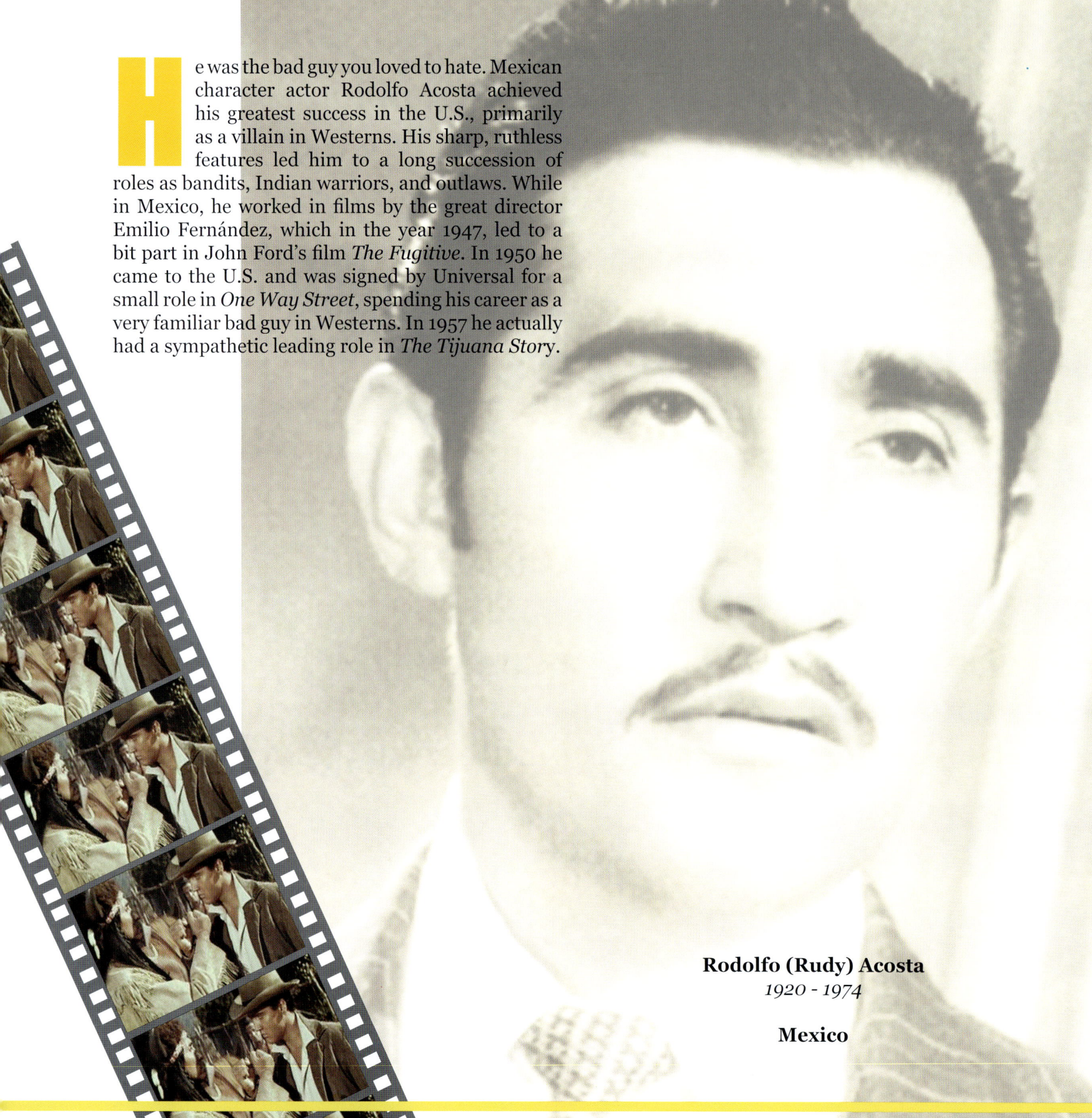

He was the bad guy you loved to hate. Mexican character actor Rodolfo Acosta achieved his greatest success in the U.S., primarily as a villain in Westerns. His sharp, ruthless features led him to a long succession of roles as bandits, Indian warriors, and outlaws. While in Mexico, he worked in films by the great director Emilio Fernández, which in the year 1947, led to a bit part in John Ford's film *The Fugitive*. In 1950 he came to the U.S. and was signed by Universal for a small role in *One Way Street*, spending his career as a very familiar bad guy in Westerns. In 1957 he actually had a sympathetic leading role in *The Tijuana Story*.

Rodolfo (Rudy) Acosta
1920 - 1974

Mexico

Given the screen name "Alvarado" by studio chief Jack Warner while driving past the Los Angeles street with that distinctively Spanish last name, Paige got his first uncredited silent film part in 1924 and played a number of subsequent starring roles that relied on his Latin good looks, achieving a certain following as a Rudolph Valentino type. The advent of talkies all but ended his starring roles, but he still managed to work regularly, usually cast as secondary Spanish characters. In 1939, using the name "Don Page" for screen credit purposes, he began working as an assistant director for Warner Bros. and then a few years later as a production manager. In these capacities he was part of the team that made a number of highly successful films, including the great Humphrey Bogart's *The Treasure of the Sierra Madre*, the young James Dean films *East of Eden* and *Rebel Without a Cause*, and his final film work, the great movie version of the Ernest Hemingway novel *The Old Man and the Sea*.

Don Alvarado / José Paige
1900/1904? - 1967

USA

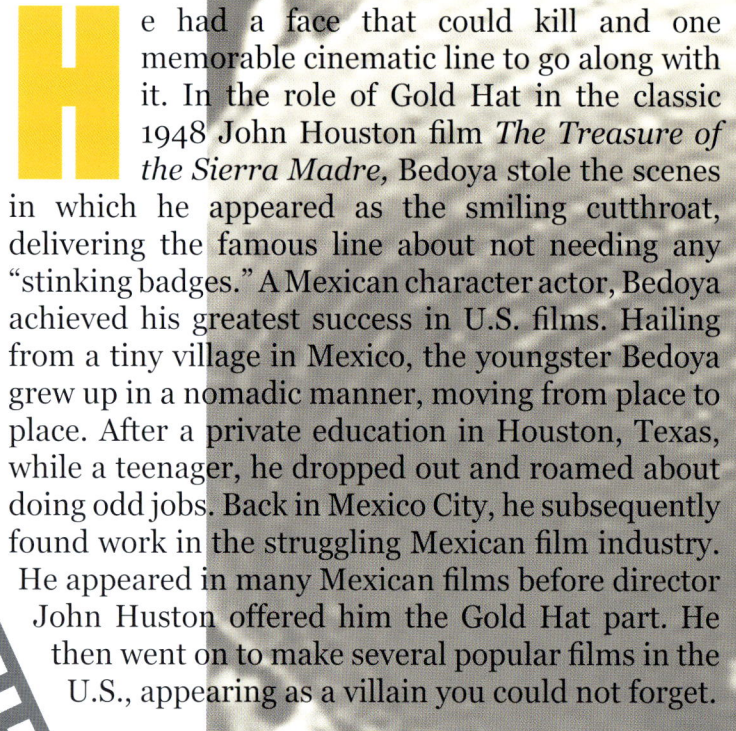

He had a face that could kill and one memorable cinematic line to go along with it. In the role of Gold Hat in the classic 1948 John Houston film *The Treasure of the Sierra Madre,* Bedoya stole the scenes in which he appeared as the smiling cutthroat, delivering the famous line about not needing any "stinking badges." A Mexican character actor, Bedoya achieved his greatest success in U.S. films. Hailing from a tiny village in Mexico, the youngster Bedoya grew up in a nomadic manner, moving from place to place. After a private education in Houston, Texas, while a teenager, he dropped out and roamed about doing odd jobs. Back in Mexico City, he subsequently found work in the struggling Mexican film industry. He appeared in many Mexican films before director John Huston offered him the Gold Hat part. He then went on to make several popular films in the U.S., appearing as a villain you could not forget.

Alfonso Bedoya
1904 - 1957

Mexico

Rafael knew that he wanted to act by the age of six, and in 1949 his dream began to unfold when his parents migrated to New York City, where he was admitted to the prestigious High School of Performing Arts. While paying his dues as an actor in New York City, he got his big break when he caught the attention of famed director Richard Brooks, who cast him in a major featured role in the now classic 1955 film *The Blackboard Jungle* (which also launched the career of the great Sidney Poitier). The film caused a major uproar upon its release, and American audiences rebelled... it contained some weird devil music called rock-and-roll. His career took off like lighting, and he was well liked by directors and casting agents, his advice being, "bring them flowers and chocolates." He appeared in over 20 films and countless television programs, and ironically, his last film, *Fever Pitch*, was directed by Richard Brooks, the man who discovered him. "...I went on a fun trip to Las Vegas with friends and came back married to Dinah Washington... it didn't last too long (smiling)..." That's how Rafael lived his life, but he never looked for publicity and didn't care about awards. He excelled in everything he put his hands on... acting, writing, painting, journalism and poetry. His last television appearance was in Tennessee William's *A Streetcar Named Desire*, which was as he once told me, his favorite of all time. He was highly honored by his countrymen with the Dominican Republic Medal of Honor for Achievement in the Arts.

Rafael Campos
1936 – 1985

Dominican Republic

Actor, preservationist and conservationist, Leo Carrillo was born in Los Angeles and, before dedicating his life to noble environmental causes, enjoyed a highly successful career as an entertainer. Leo, who worked with the very biggest stars in the Hollywood galaxy during his time in the limelight, appeared in 15 major stage plays (several on Broadway) and more than 90 motion pictures in which he was featured in supporting or character roles. Leo's greatest fame came from his portrayal of Pancho, the mischievous sidekick to Duncan Renaldo's Cisco Kid in the pioneering television series of the early 1950s.

Leo Carrillo
(1880 - 1961)

USA

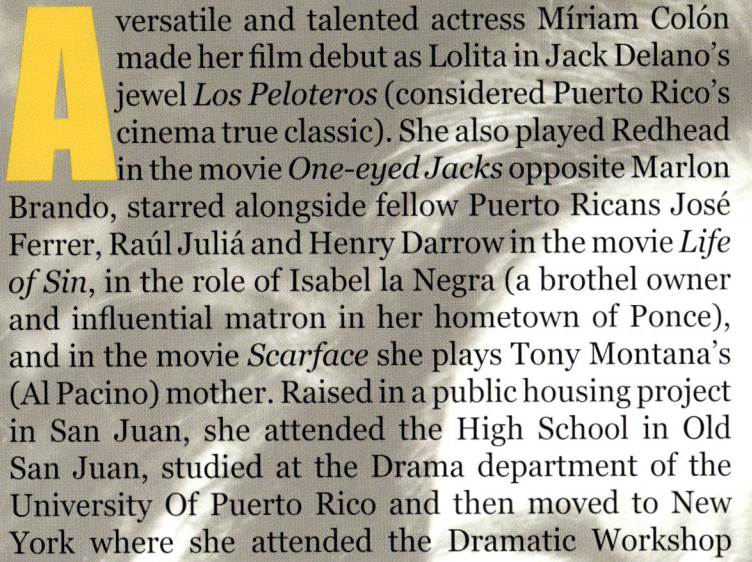

A versatile and talented actress Míriam Colón made her film debut as Lolita in Jack Delano's jewel *Los Peloteros* (considered Puerto Rico's cinema true classic). She also played Redhead in the movie *One-eyed Jacks* opposite Marlon Brando, starred alongside fellow Puerto Ricans José Ferrer, Raúl Juliá and Henry Darrow in the movie *Life of Sin*, in the role of Isabel la Negra (a brothel owner and influential matron in her hometown of Ponce), and in the movie *Scarface* she plays Tony Montana's (Al Pacino) mother. Raised in a public housing project in San Juan, she attended the High School in Old San Juan, studied at the Drama department of the University Of Puerto Rico and then moved to New York where she attended the Dramatic Workshop and Technical Institute and The Lee Strasberg Acting Studio. A favorite of TV Westerns, from 1954 to 1974, Colón made over 250 guest appearances in television shows, she played Maria Santos a recurring role in the American soap opera *Guiding Light*. It is reported that a presentation of René Marqués's *La Carreta* (*The Oxcart*) motivated her to form the first Hispanic theater group. Miriam is the artistic director of the Puerto Rican Traveling Theater that she founded in 1969, which has produced more than 100 different plays. Besides her work with the Puerto Rican Traveling Theater, she is still active in Broadway and off-Broadway stages.

Míriam Colón Valle
1936

Puerto Rico

Mapy, who was Puerto Rican and not Mexican (as many people thought), became a famous actress south of the border, during the Mexican film industry's golden era. Acting since an early age, she arrived in Mexico in the early 1930s, where she met and married the already famous Puerto Rican actor and producer Fernando Cortés, who had already adopted Mexican citizenship. Making her debut in the movie *Dos Mujeres y un Don Juan* (*Two Women and a Womanizer*), she then went on to star in over 50 films in Mexico and in Puerto Rico. A phenomenon across Latin America, during the decade of the 1940s, she starred in movies in practically every Latin American country that had a film industry. Gaining celebrity status in places like Cuba and Argentina, she starred in movies that are considered classics among those produced in those countries. Mapy, who was also a comedian and a musical theatre actress, parlayed her acting career into a singing one, recording various albums while still active as an actress. She and her husband Fernando returned to the Island and presented an idea for a comedy show and on March 28, 1954, Puerto Rico received its first television transmission. The first comedy show to go on the air was "Mapy Y Papi" which also included Maria Judith Franco and Paquito Cordero, Mapy's nephew, himself a legendary figure in Puerto Rican show-business.

Mapy Cortés / María del Pilar Cordero
(1910 – 1998)

Puerto Rico

Many believe that Cugat had more to do with the infusion of Latin music into United States popular music than any other musician. The Catalan-Cuban bandleader was born in Girona, Spain, and his family emigrated to Cuba when he was five. Trained as a classical violinist, he played with the Orchestra of the Teatro Nacional in Havana. In 1915, Cugat and his family arrived in New York. Entering the world of show business, he played with a band called The Gigolos during the tango craze. Later, he went to work for the *Los Angeles Times* as a caricaturist. By the early 1930s, he began appearing with his group in feature films. Cugat took his band to open the new Waldorf Astoria Hotel, and it became the hotel's resident group. The song "Perfidia," which he recorded in 1940 with Cuban singer Miguelito Valdés, became a major hit. Cugat followed trends closely, making records for the conga, the mambo, the cha-cha-cha and the twist when each was in fashion. He married salsa dancer Charo in 1966; the two were the first couple to marry in the newly opened Caesar's Palace in Las Vegas.

**Xavier Cugat /
Francesc d'Asís Xavier Cugat Mingall de Bru i Deulofeu**
1900 - 1990

Spain

Bebe Daniels / Phyllis Daniels
1901 - 1971

USA

Half Irish and half Mexican, Bebe started out in Hollywood in the silent movie era and later starred on radio and television in England. Bebe began her acting career at the age of four and had her first starring role in film by the age of seven as the young heroine in *A Common Enemy*. At the age of 14 she starred opposite famous film comedian Harold Lloyd in a series of *Lonesome Luke* two-reel comedies. Bebe is also believed to be the second actress to appear on screen as the character of Dorothy Gale, in the 1910 film short *The Wonderful Wizard of Oz*. For a time she went by the name Virginia Daniels, and in 1924 she played opposite the great Rudolph Valentino in *Monsieur Beaucaire*. A huge hit in the 1929 talkie Rio Rita, in which she stunned audiences by singing so well, the film proved to be one of the most successful films of that year, and RCA Victor even hired her to record several records for their catalog. She was awarded the Medal of Freedom by Harry S. Truman for war service, and with her husband, son and daughter, she starred in the radio sitcom *Life With The Lyons*, which later made the transition to television.

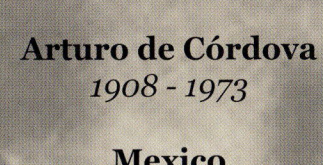

Arturo de Córdova
1908 - 1973

Mexico

Entering the Mexican film industry in the 1930s, it didn't take Arturo de Córdova long to become a major star, specializing in action and adventure films. His memorable portrayal in 1951 of an insane aristocrat in Luis Bunuel's *El* remains his greatest acting achievement. Paramount Pictures never gave up hope of discovering and nurturing a new "Latin lover" type after losing Rudolph Valentino in a 1924 contract dispute, so the studio signed the popular Mexican actor to a Hollywood contract in 1943. De Córdova was showcased in the small but memorable role of Augustín in Paramount's *For Whom the Bell Tolls*, then starred in a handful of subsequent features. Returning to Mexico in the late 1940s, de Córdova continued to appear in Latin American films, eventually surpassing his previous fame by also becoming a major star in South America and Spain, until his premature retirement in the early 1950s.

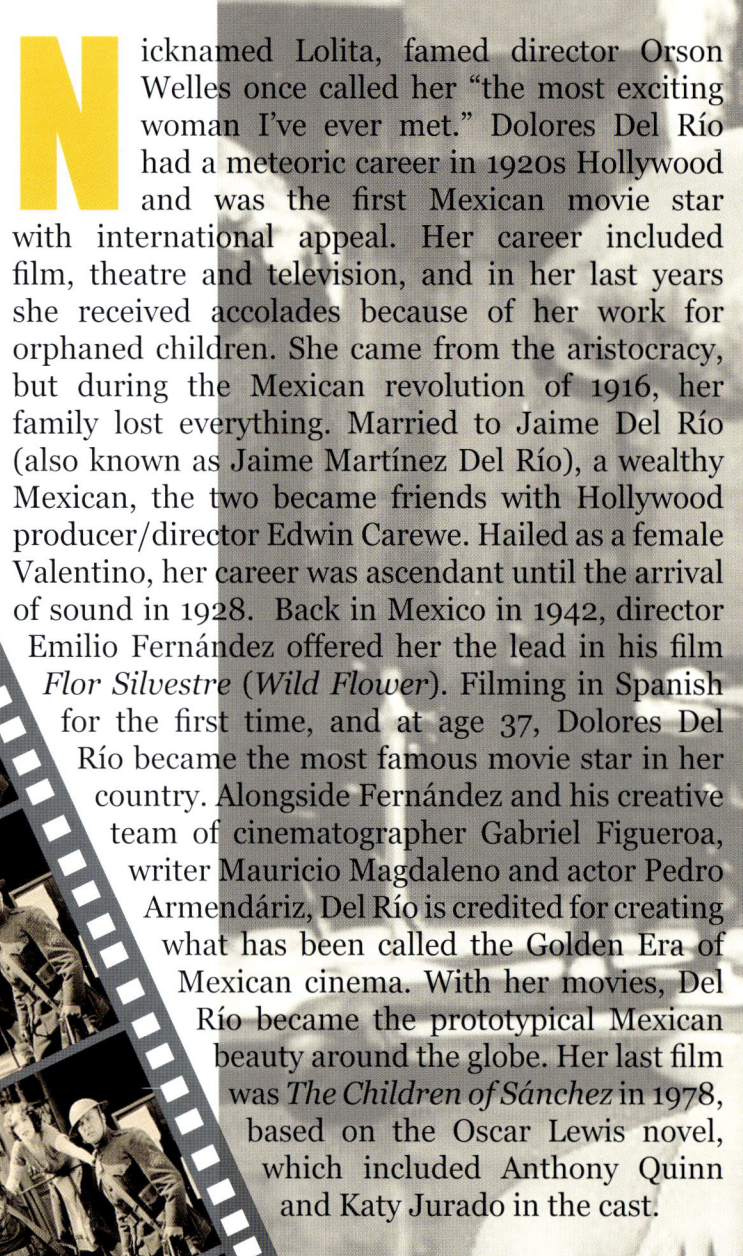

Nicknamed Lolita, famed director Orson Welles once called her "the most exciting woman I've ever met." Dolores Del Río had a meteoric career in 1920s Hollywood and was the first Mexican movie star with international appeal. Her career included film, theatre and television, and in her last years she received accolades because of her work for orphaned children. She came from the aristocracy, but during the Mexican revolution of 1916, her family lost everything. Married to Jaime Del Río (also known as Jaime Martínez Del Río), a wealthy Mexican, the two became friends with Hollywood producer/director Edwin Carewe. Hailed as a female Valentino, her career was ascendant until the arrival of sound in 1928. Back in Mexico in 1942, director Emilio Fernández offered her the lead in his film *Flor Silvestre* (*Wild Flower*). Filming in Spanish for the first time, and at age 37, Dolores Del Río became the most famous movie star in her country. Alongside Fernández and his creative team of cinematographer Gabriel Figueroa, writer Mauricio Magdaleno and actor Pedro Armendáriz, Del Río is credited for creating what has been called the Golden Era of Mexican cinema. With her movies, Del Río became the prototypical Mexican beauty around the globe. Her last film was *The Children of Sánchez* in 1978, based on the Oscar Lewis novel, which included Anthony Quinn and Katy Jurado in the cast.

Dolores Del Río /
Dolores Martínez Asúnsolo y López Negrete
1905 - 1983

Mexico

Héctor Elizondo
1936

USA

An accomplished athlete, dancer, singer, guitarist and bongo player, this Newyorker of Basque and Puerto Rican descent has also achieved a lot in the acting arena. This talented film and television star was discovered at an early age by the legendary W.C. Handy. He attended public school, took voice lessons, studied dance at the Ballet Arts Company at Carnegie Hall and since 1970 his credit has appeared in more than 130 movies and TV-movies and serials. His first major success came playing God disguised as a Puerto Rican steam room attendant in Bruce Jay Friedman's *Steambath*. While the play itself got mixed reviews, his performance was praised by the critics and he won an Obie award for his efforts. In Garry Marshall's 1990 film *Pretty Woman*, alongside Hollywood mega-stars Richard Gere and Julia Roberts, Elizondo got a Golden Globe award nomination for best supporting actor for a character that appears on screen for about 10 minutes. The television series *Chicago Hope* during the mid 90s and a variety of work in films and television solidified his reputation as a character actor who is able to play just about every conceivable role.

Academy Award winner José Ferrer was a versatile actor. He has played everything from a hypnotist to a dictator; he teamed with John Houston for the realistic portrayal of the famous French artist Toulouse Lautrec in *Moulin Rouge*; fittingly director David Lynch cast Ferrer in *Dune* as The Emperor. In *Twentieth Century* he performed with Gloria Swanson and accepted roles in Billy Wilder's *Fedora* and Woody Allen's *A Midsummer Night's Dream*. His body of work also includes the epic *Lawrence of Arabia*, *Ship of Fools* and *The Caine Mutiny*. He studied architecture at Princeton, but he discovered theatre in his final year and started acting, never to stop again. In 1943, he played Iago opposite to Paul Robeson's *Othello* on Broadway. Soon he was directing and starring in the stage production of *Cyrano de Bergerac*, a portrayal he took to the big screen, which nabbed him an Oscar in 1950 for best actor, thus making him the first Latino to be so honored in that category.

**José Ferrer /
José Vicente Ferrer de Otero y Cintrón**
1912 - 1992

Puerto Rico

By virtue of his weight, his raspy voice and his baleful appearance, Gómez was often cast as heavies, though he evinced a preference for characters with "some rascality, warmth and dimension." Awarded a scholarship to a prestigious New York drama school at 17, Thomas Gómez began his acting career in theatre during the 1920s and was a student of the actor Walter Hampden. Gómez first stepped on the Broadway stage as a cadet in Walter Hampden's *Cyrano de Bergerac*. He made his first film *Sherlock Holmes and the Voice of Terror* in 1942 and by the end of his career had appeared in 60 films. In 1947 he received a nomination for an Academy Award for best supporting actor for his performance in the film *Ride the Pink Horse*. Of Spanish heritage, Gómez refused to play Latin characters unless they could be presented "with sympathy, or at least with humanity." Amidst his dramatic roles, Gómez proved a worthy foil to such comedians as Bob Hope and Abbott and Costello.

**Thomas Gómez /
Sabino Tomás Gómez**

1905 – 1971

USA

She was an amazingly talented dancer and actress, as well as a beautiful woman on top of it all. The daughter of professional dancers, Eduardo and Volga, she became her father's dance partner at the age of 12 and by the tender age of 13, she was dancing in hot spots in Tijuana. Few beauties can come close to the radiance she brings to the screen. The characters she played were fiery to the point of self-destruction. This was never so evident as in the film *Gilda*, her most notable performance. Always a dancer, in *You'll Never Get Rich* and *You Were Never Lovelier*, Rita danced with the ever-popular Fred Astaire. *In Cover Girl*, she danced up a storm with Gene Kelly. After being featured in *Blood and Sand*, her roles as film goddess and seductress became the parts she lived up to in her real life, enjoying a formidable string of lovers and husbands. After a short marriage to Orson Welles, who directed her in *The Lady from Shanghai*, Rita married Prince Aly Khan and left Hollywood. But before long she was divorced, back in Hollywood, and starring in the films *Salome* and *Miss Sadie Thompson*. Married again, this time to an abusive man, a singer named Dick Haymes, she was absent for a short while but came back three years later, giving critically acclaimed performances in *Fire Down Below* in 1957 and *Separate Tables* the next year. Married again, this time to film producer, James Hill, she finally also divorced him in 1961.

**Rita Hayworth /
Margarita Cansino**
1918 - 1987

Mexico

Hernandez was one of the first "new style" black screen actors, who neither sang nor danced but played characters just as white actors did. He specialized in masculine, sensitive, individualistic men. Born in San Juan, Puerto Rico, to a Puerto Rican fisherman and a Brazilian mother, he grew up as an orphan in the streets of Rio de Janeiro. He first began performing on stage in an acrobatic act. He also worked as a professional boxer under the name Kid Curley and went on to work in a minstrel show, in circuses and in vaudeville. He made his debut on Broadway in 1927 in *Show Boat*, played a few bit parts in the films of Oscar Micheaux, and also worked as a radio scriptwriter. Hernandez participated in 23 films throughout his career and broke through as a screen actor in 1949 with *Intruder in the Dust*, in which he played a proud black man wrongly accused of having killed a white Southerner. The film earned him a Golden Globe nomination for most promising male newcomer. He continued acting until shortly before his death, working in both films and on TV.

**Juano Hernández /
Huano G. Hernández**
1896/1901? - 1970

Puerto Rico

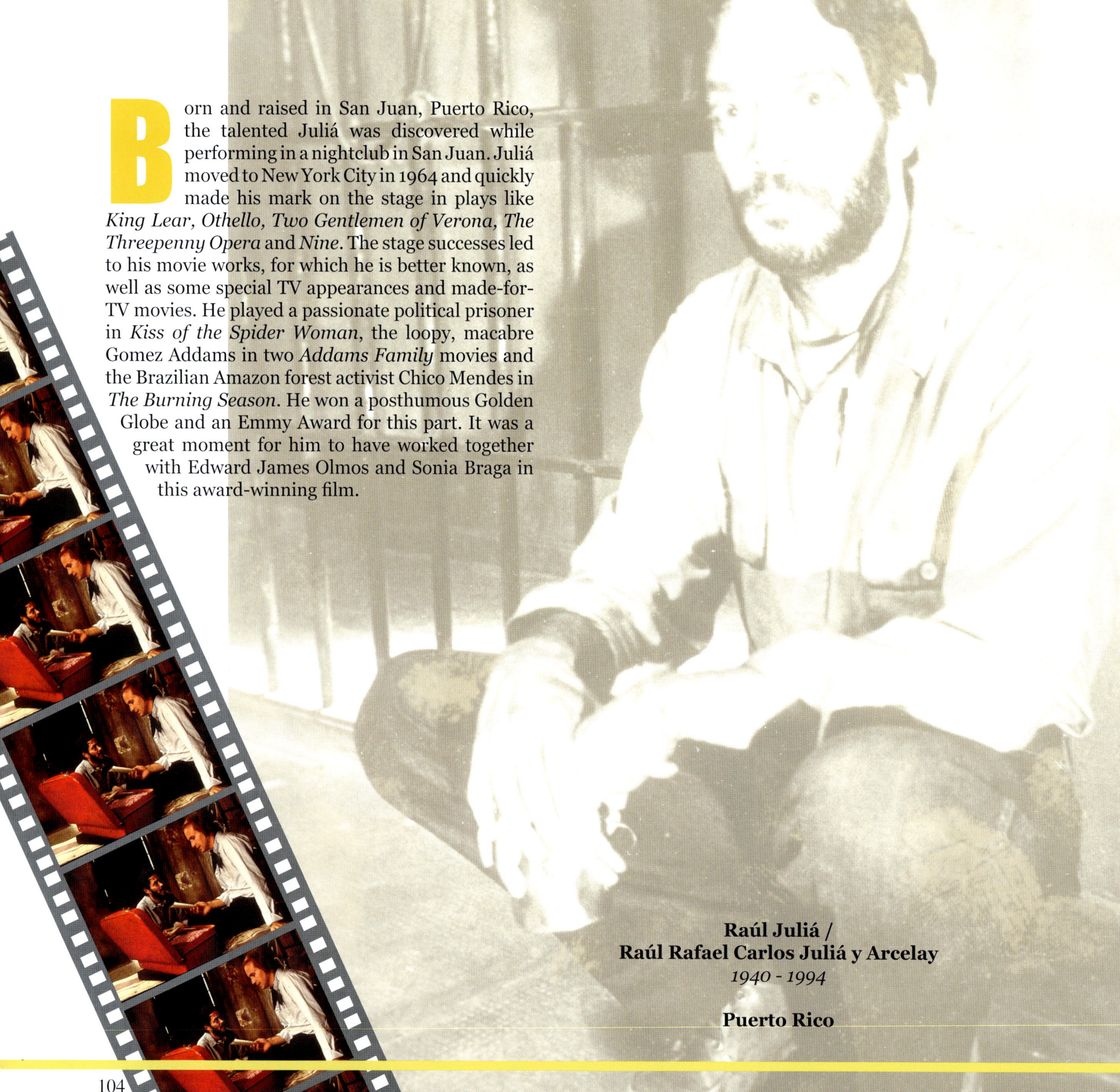

Born and raised in San Juan, Puerto Rico, the talented Juliá was discovered while performing in a nightclub in San Juan. Juliá moved to New York City in 1964 and quickly made his mark on the stage in plays like *King Lear, Othello, Two Gentlemen of Verona, The Threepenny Opera* and *Nine*. The stage successes led to his movie works, for which he is better known, as well as some special TV appearances and made-for-TV movies. He played a passionate political prisoner in *Kiss of the Spider Woman*, the loopy, macabre Gomez Addams in two *Addams Family* movies and the Brazilian Amazon forest activist Chico Mendes in *The Burning Season*. He won a posthumous Golden Globe and an Emmy Award for this part. It was a great moment for him to have worked together with Edward James Olmos and Sonia Braga in this award-winning film.

**Raúl Juliá /
Raúl Rafael Carlos Juliá y Arcelay**
1940 - 1994

Puerto Rico

Sexy and exotic, her luscious lips and full-bodied figure were provocative and alluring, but her eyes spoke of a deep sincerity. Not limited to being a sex goddess, her persona also allowed her to be portrayed in Hollywood as a woman of distinction. Katy Jurado's performances included work with Gary Cooper, Karl Malden, Albert Finney, Gilbert Roland, Marlon Brando, Anthony Quinn and César Romero. Her roles often required she play a person of great fortitude, tenderness and self-respect. Jurado was an Oscar nominee for her supporting role in the film, *Broken Lance,* and many people feel she was cheated out of an Oscar nomination for her performance in the popular, award-winning Western *High Noon*.

**Katy Jurado /
María Cristina Estela Marcela Jurado García**
1927 - 2002

Mexico

Even though he lives on in popular culture thanks to "Fernando," a character developed by Billy Crystal on *Saturday Night Live* in the mid-1980s, in reality Fernando Lamas was already an established movie star in his native Argentina when he signed a contract with Metro-Goldwyn-Mayer in 1951. Once in the United States, Lamas played the then popular Latin lover roles. A sought-after romantic lead, Lamas directed his first film project in 1963, a Spanish movie titled *Magic Fountain* starring his wife Esther Williams, and after more than a decade in front of the Hollywood lens he went on to become a busy director. Most active in television series like *Mannix*, *The Violent Ones*, *Alias Smith and Jones*, *Starsky and Hutch* and *Falcon Crest* (the latter co-starred by his son, Lorenzo) he kept working in front and behind the camera up to the time of his untimely death due to pancreatic cancer.

**Fernando Lamas/
Fernando Álvaro Lamas y de Santos**
1915-1982

Argentina

Described as a "Tough-talking American character actor" by All Movie Guide's Hal Erickson, Perry López has been playing "ethnic" roles since he made his screen debut in *The Creature from the Black Lagoon* in 1954 in an uncredited appearance. López, born and raised in New York City, soon after signed a contract with Warner Bros. and went on to play supporting roles in several 1950s classics like *Mister Roberts*, *The McConnell Story* and *The Violent Road*. He is best remembered as police officer Lou Escobar in Roman Polanski's *Chinatown* and its sequel *The Two Jakes*, with Escobar now a police captain. Trekkies around the globe know him as Star Fleet's botanist Esteban Rodríguez. Unlike Ricardo Montalbán's appearance in the Star Trek series (Khan was an otherworldly alien) López played a character that was a real Hispanic scientist traveling the galaxy aboard the USS Enterprise.

Perry López
1931 - 2008

USA

**Mona Maris /
Mona María Emita Cap de Vielle**
1903 - 1991

Argentina

It is said that while living in Germany, the young actress was given a screen test during which the camera was not loaded with film, but a prominent director noticed Maris and offered her a five-year contract. The daughter of a Spanish Basque mother and a French Basque father, and educated in England, France and Germany, Mona spoke four languages, and her ambition to become an actress originated during World War I, when she was a pupil in Luders, France. Joe Schenck, president of United Artists, granted her the prospect of a Hollywood career. Known in her native land as the "Pride of the Pampas," she arrived at the United Artists studio in 1928 when she was 20 years old. Maris' film career began with the 1925 silent movie *The Apache* and continued until the 1980s. Her last appearance was in *Camila* in 1984.

Nicknamed Carmen by her father because of his love of opera (specifically *Carmen* by Bizet), she later became famous as The Brazilian Bombshell. Often shown wearing platform sandals and towering headdresses made of fruit, she also became famous as "the lady in the tutti-frutti hat." Carmen Miranda was born in a small northern Portuguese town, but shortly after her birth, her family emigrated to Brazil and settled in Rio de Janeiro (the then capital). In her spare time, she often sang at parties and festivals around town, but her very Catholic parents did not approve of her dreams of pursuing a career in show business, so she kept her plans secret for years. Eventually discovered and given the chance to perform on a local radio station, she had a 10-year career as a samba singer before she was invited to New York City to perform in a show on Broadway. A noted musical innovator in Brazil, she was one of the first samba superstars and made six films during her career in Brazil before her arrival in the United States in 1939 with her band, *Bando da Lua*, achieving stardom in the early 1940s. She was the country's highest-paid entertainer for several years in the 1940s, and in 1945 she was the highest paid woman in the United States earning more than $200,000. Miranda made a total of 14 Hollywood films between 1940 and 1953. As a singer, she sold more than 10 million records worldwide.

**Carmen Miranda /
Maria do Carmo Miranda Da Cunha**
1909 - 1955

Portugal

His distinctive Spanish accent (especially in his car commercials in which he seductively exhorted the pleasures of fine upholstery) made him an American icon. Ideally tall, dark, and handsome, the curly haired Ricardo Montalbán once played romantic leads in major features of the 40s and 50s. He spent part of his youth in the U.S. and worked as a bit player on Broadway before returning to his native Mexico in the early '40s to launch what would become a fruitful film career. Best remembered for playing the mysterious Mr. Roarke on the popular television series *Fantasy Island* (1978-1984), and for his intense portrayal of Khan Noonien Singh, in both the television series and the second film version of the popular *Star Trek* franchise, he also had a successful career on-stage. Often cast in ethnic roles, Montalbán penned his biography titled "Reflections: A Life in Two Worlds" in 1980 and, even though confined to a wheelchair after a spinal operation, Montalbán continues to play an active role in promoting Nosotros — a non-profit organization founded by him in 1970 and dedicated to improving the image of Latinos within the entertainment industry. Montalbán's career has been revived during recent years as the actor began performing voice-over work on a series of animated films and television shows. The role as the grandfather in Robert Rodriguez's *Spy Kids 2: Island of Lost Dreams* and *Spy Kids 3-D: Game Over*, giving the actor an opportunity to rise once again thanks to the magic of special effects.

**Ricardo Montalbán /
Ricardo Gonzalo Pedro Montalbán Merino**
1920

Mexico

María Móntez / María Antonia Vidal de Santos Silas y Gracia
1920 - 1953

Dominican Republic

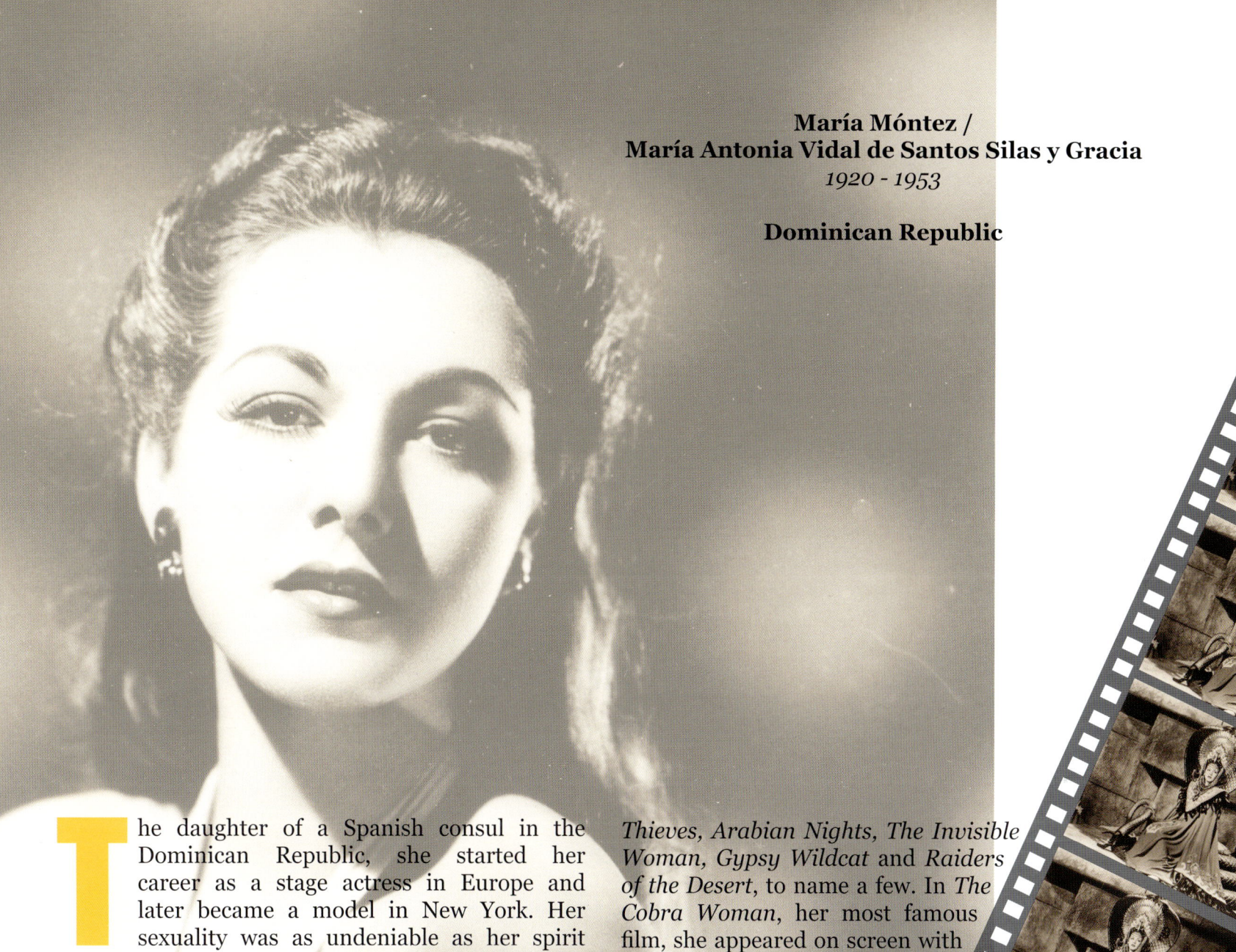

The daughter of a Spanish consul in the Dominican Republic, she started her career as a stage actress in Europe and later became a model in New York. Her sexuality was as undeniable as her spirit was indomitable, yet "The Queen of Technicolor" Móntez always maintained a regal presence no matter the role. Universal recognized her ability to capture the imagination of the audience, building enormous thrones and other appropriate furniture for her to drape herself across. Her pictures were often exotic, grand and highly profitable color adventures. She appeared in *White Savage* with Jon Hall, Sidney Toler and Sabu. In *Siren of Atlantis* she performed with her French husband, Jean-Pierre Aumont, and in *Pirates of Monterey* she played opposite the handsome and well-favored Gilbert Roland. A popular adventure heroine she starred in films like *Ali Baba and the Forty Thieves, Arabian Nights, The Invisible Woman, Gypsy Wildcat* and *Raiders of the Desert*, to name a few. In *The Cobra Woman*, her most famous film, she appeared on screen with Lon Chaney Jr. and played twin sisters: one good, one evil. In one scene, María performs the ritual of the cobra dance, the pinnacle of her career. Her death at the age of 33, is still a mystery today. It was reported that she died from a heart attack while taking a hot bath.

Sara was her grandmother's first name and Montiel was a tribute to her hometown Campos de Montiel (Fields of Montiel). Signed in her teens to a long-term movie contract as a reward after she won a beauty and talent contest, she made her debut in the film *Te Quiero Para Mí* (*I Want You for Myself*). But the young actress caught the attention of producers and directors, which led to starring roles and a new image and a new name. Her first international success *Locura de Amor* (*Crazy from Love*) led to a long term contract in Mexico and then Hollywood producers won her over for their films. Formally introduced to American moviegoers in *Vera Cruz* opposite Gary Cooper and Burt Lancaster, later she starred in *Serenade* with Mario Lanza, Joan Fontaine and Vincent Price, and *The Run of the Arrow* with Rod Steiger, Brian Keith and Charles Bronson. Back in Spain she starred in *El Último Cuplé* (*The Last Song*) and Montiel became a national treasure. Winner two years in a row of the *Premio del Sindicato* (Spain's equivalent to the Hollywood Oscar), for her performances in *El Último Cuplé* and *La Violetera* (*The Violet Peddler*), the soundtrack albums from both films reportedly outsold Presley and Sinatra in the world market. After a retrospective of her career ran at the Autumn Film Festival in Paris, she published her memoirs *Vivir es un placer* (*To Live Is a Pleasure*). After breaking up a short romance with Italian actor Giancarlo Viola, the star began a controversial relationship with 38-year-old Tony Hernandez, a Cuban videotape operator residing in Havana, marrying him in Madrid in 2002 and filing for divorce the next year.

**Sara Montiel /
María Antonia Alejandra Abad y Fernández**
1928

Spain

A highly regarded matinee idol and a notable film director of the silent film era who worked up to the 1950s, his film career spanned more than four decades. Born in Madrid, Moreno emigrated to the United States at the age of 14 and settled in Massachusetts, where he completed his education. In 1912, he was signed to Vitagraph Studios and began his career in bit parts and as a movie extra. Often typecast in his earliest films as the "Latin lover," as were other actors of the era with Latin roots, in 1914 Moreno began co-starring in a series of highly successful serials opposite the popular silent film actress Pearl White. He became an overnight sensation and played opposite the biggest stars of the time. Moreno's career began to falter with the advent of talkies, partly because of his heavy Spanish accent. Relocating to Mexico, Moreno directed several well-received Mexican films. His 1932 drama *Santa* has been hailed by film critics as one of the best Mexican films of the era. By the mid-1930s, Antonio Moreno began rebuilding his faltering Hollywood career by taking notable roles as a character actor and went on to appear in a number of box office hits.

Antonio "Tony" Moreno / Antonio Garride Monteagudo
1887 - 1967

Spain

Described as "the world's greatest comedian" by none other than Charles Chaplin, his routine consisted of engaging in drawn-out, nonsensical chatter. Cantinflas is responsible for more than one word in the modern Spanish language dictionary, including the verb "cantinflear," which roughly means to talk a lot but say nothing of substance. Cantinflas, a prolific and productive Mexican comedian/producer/writer/singer died a millionaire several times over and was one of the biggest stars ever in Spanish-language films, but he never forgot where he came from. Much of his money was given over to charitable work, including high-quality, low-income housing for Mexico City's poor. When he died, he was hailed as a national hero, and a protracted period of official mourning followed. He appeared in more than 55 films, including the part of Passepartoute in the extravagant Hollywood epic *Around the World in Eighty Days* in 1956 and *Pepe*, in which he shares the screen with a slew of international stars of the time.

Mario Moreno (Cantinflas) / Mario Moreno Reyes
1911 - 1993

Mexico

She is a very talented and productive singer, dancer, Academy Award-winning actress and already a true Hollywood legend. Rita Moreno is one of only nine people (the second actor, and the first Hispanic) to have won an Emmy, a Grammy, an Oscar, and a Tony award. Moreno, who moved with her mother to New York City at the age of five, lent her voice to Spanish-language versions of American films by the time she was eleven years old, and had her first speaking role by the time she was thirteen. Boxed in roles which she considered degrading, she has fought the negative depiction of Latinos in Hollywood all her life. Awarded the Presidential Medal of Freedom in 2004, Moreno's main contribution to the Hispanic community has been her ability to transcend what some have viewed as the widespread discriminatory practices of Hollywood.

Rita Moreno / Rosita Dolores Alverío
1931

Puerto Rico

Ramón Novarro moved with his family to Los Angeles to escape the Mexican Revolution. A cousin of actress Dolores Del Río, he entered films in 1917 playing bit parts and supplemented his income by working as a singing waiter. The director Rex Ingram and his wife, the actress Alice Terry, began to promote him as a rival to Rudolph Valentino and Ingram suggested he change his name to "Novarro." From 1923 he began to play more prominent roles. His roles in *Scaramouche* and later on in *Ben-Hur*, which caused a sensation with his revealing costumes, made him a Hollywood superstar of the Silent Era. While at the peak of his success in the late 1920s and early 1930s, he was earning more than $100,000 per film. Elevated into the Hollywood elite after Valentino's death in 1926, he became the screen's leading Latin lover. Popular as a swashbuckler in action roles, he was also considered one of the great romantic lead actors of his day. Novarro continued to act sporadically, appearing in a couple of films in Mexico and France, and later in the 1940s he had several small roles in American films. He kept busy doing television until his violent death in the Hollywood hills on HALLOWEEN night in 1968 at the age of 69.

**Ramón Novarro /
José Ramón Gil Samaniego**
1899 – 1968

Mexico

His Lieutenant Martín Castillo, the top cop of the very popular television series Miami Vice, made him a staple of 1980s imagery; he played El Pachuco, the strutting, posing, super macho narrator in *Zoot Suit*, and his performance as Gaff in the modern Hollywood classic *Blade Runner*, alongside Harison Ford, is part of a prestigious Hollywood science fiction legacy. A young talented ball player (he became the Golden State batting champion), it is said that the ambitious youth taught himself to sing and play piano and formed his own rock band while still in school. An established movie star, accomplished stage and television performer, as well as a film director and passionate humanitarian with an amazing career in Hollywood and across America, he has won numerous acting and humanitarian awards and keeps on working very hard, both as a director and actor.

Edward James Olmos
1947

USA

He could, and did, play just about every part thrown his way. He was one of the few actors to move easily and successfully between starring and supporting roles throughout his career. In both categories, the Irish-Mexican Quinn portrayed a vast variety of characters and ethnicity, including American, Arab, Basque, Chinese, English, French, Greek, Hawaiian, Hebrew, Hun, Irish, Italian, Mexican, Mongol, Native American, Filipino, Portuguese, Spanish and Ukrainian. And before he launched his acting career, Quinn worked odd jobs as a butcher, a boxer, street corner preacher and slaughterhouse worker. He also won a scholarship to study architecture with Frank Lloyd Wright, with whom he developed a close relationship, at the great architect's studio in Arizona. The son of an Irish-Mexican father and an ethnic Mexican mother, his family moved from Mexico to Los Angeles, where he grew up in the barrios of Boyle Heights and Echo Park. Quinn, playing opposite Marlon Brando, won the Best Supporting Actor Academy Award for *Viva Zapata* in 1952, making him the first Mexican-American to win an Oscar. He won his second Best Supporting Oscar in 1957 for his portrayal of Paul Gauguin in *Lust for Life*, a movie in which he only appeared on screen for a total of eight minutes. He received his third Oscar nomination (and first for Best Actor) for George Cukor's *Wild Is the Wind*. And the part of *Zorba the Greek* in the 1964 film of the same name brought him his fourth, and last, Oscar nomination. The consummate film performer, who appeared in so many great movies, was also a talented painter and an accomplished stage actor, appearing on Broadway in the leading role of Stanley Kowalski in Tennessee Williams's *A Streetcar Named Desire* and then later receiving outstanding reviews for his performance in the stage version of *Zorba*.

**Anthony Quinn /
Antonio Rudolfo Oaxaca Quinn**
1915 - 2001

Mexico

**Duncan Renaldo /
Renault Renaldo Duncan**
1904 – 1980

Spain

He was a producer, writer and director; his portrayal of the Cisco Kid on early American television is part of the nation's cultural heritage. Not sure himself where he had been born, though his earliest memories were of Spain, Renaldo never knew his biological parents and was raised in several European countries. Emigrated to America in the 1920s and after failing to earn a living as a portrait painter, he tried producing short films. He eventually took up acting and signed with MGM in 1928. Arrested in 1934 for illegal entry into the United States, he was pardoned by President Franklin Roosevelt and returned to acting. Widely used in the B-film genre, he was also credited in big budgeted movies as well, including roles opposite stars like George Raft, Henry Fonda, John Barrymore, Gary Cooper and Ingrid Bergman. Renaldo also illustrated a book of poetry by Moreton B. Price titled "Drifter's Dreams." For his contributions to the television industry, Duncan Renaldo has a star on the Hollywood Walk of Fame at 1680 Vine Street.

Rey was born in Buenos Aires and became famous as an actor in Argentine movies before making the decision to emigrate to the United States in 1960, and in 1967, became a naturalized citizen. He was most famous for his roles in movies like *Fun in Acapulco* with Elvis Presley (1963), as well as the lead in *The Stepmother* (1972). On television, he was most famous for his role as Carlos Ramírez in *The Flying Nun*, a part he played from 1967 to 1970. He went on to play Karl Duval on *Days of Our Lives* from 1976 to 1977. His solid performance as the Russian immigrant who was Robin Williams's attorney/protector in *Moscow on the Hudson* in 1984, was a major highlight in his career. He was married to Joyce Bowman in 1969, and they had one son. He died in Los Angeles of lung cancer and was interred in the Holy Cross Cemetery in Culver City, California.

Alejandro Rey
1930 – 1987

Argentina

Famous as the French villain Alain Charnier in William Friedkin's *The French Connection* (1971), Fernando Rey is considered the first "international Spanish actor." Consolidating his well deserved fame as Spain's premier actor, Rey is credited as acting in four different film versions of Don Quixote in different roles, if one counts the 1992 re-dubbed version of Orson Welles' *Don Quixote*. His work with Luis Buñuel during the 1960s and 1970s made him internationally famous in both Europe and the United States. Rey started to study architecture when the Spanish Civil War began cutting his student days short. In 1936, he began his career in movies as an extra, sometimes even getting credited with his stage name (he took his mother's second surname Rey, Spanish for "King"). With a prolific career in movies, radio, theater and television, he was also a great dubbing actor in Spanish television. With a voice that was "considered intense and personal," Rey is heard as the narrator of some of the most important Spanish movies like Luis García Berlanga's *Bienvenido Mr. Marshall* (1953) and Ladislao Vajda's *Marcelino Pan y Vino* (*Marcelino Bread and Wine*) (1955).

**Fernando Rey /
Fernando Casado D'Arambillet**
1917 – 1994

Spain

Tall, suave and sophisticated, he believed in living well and in dressing well. It is reported that his closets held 30 tuxedos, 200 sports jackets and 500 suits. Born of Cuban parents in New York City, his maternal grandfather was the Cuban poet-patriot José Martí, and his first work was as a ballroom dancer. Better known to younger generations as the white-faced, green-haired, cackling villain The Joker of the campy television series *Batman*, that was actually only a small part of the enormous amount of work that Romero contributed to television (he had guest-starred in dozens of television shows) and in films, such as his role as the bumbling corporate villain chasing a young Kurt Russell in the Walt Disney comedies like *The Computer Wore Tennis Shoes*. But to older audiences, he was a distinguished Latin lover in a great number of musicals and romantic comedies and played the rogue bandit *The Cisco Kid*. He was a versatile star in an overwhelming variety of roles in a career as an actor, dancer and comedian that lasted nearly 60 years.

Cesar Romero / César Julio Romero Jr.
1907 - 1994

USA

Gilbert Roland played opposite a number of name actresses who were the divas of their time including Barbara Stanwyk, Lana Turner, Jane Russell and Bette Davis. His family witnessed the attack of General Villa on their town. His father, a well-respected bullfighter, was paralyzed and later died from the wounds inflicted by the bulls he fought. Roland's start included bullfighting opposite Valentino in *Blood and Sand*. Later on in his career he again appeared as a bullfighter in *The Bullfighter and The Lady*, Roland's self-professed favorite film. Katy Jurado plays his wife, and the two give a performance based on love, honor and mutual respect. He landed his first star appearance as Armand Duval in *Camille* opposite the great Norma Talmadge. But it was in *The Dove* that Gilbert Roland became one of the first true Latin lovers of the screen. His dark curly hair and eloquent eyes created a heartthrob whose pulse can still be felt. Roland also appeared in *Seahawks* with Errol Flynn, *Juarez* with Paul Muni, and *Ten Tall Men* with Burt Lancaster. This span of roles from macho to lover, fool to soldier made it impossible to typecast Roland. In *The Miracle of Our Lady of Fatima*, he played a scoundrel; in *The Bad and The Beautiful*, he's the quintessential Latin lover; and in *Barbarosa*, Roland is a man of courage, loyal to his family and his people. Even the legendary John Huston cast him in the successful and critically acclaimed *We Were Strangers* in 1949. Houston was blacklisted as a communist sympathizer following the release of the film.

**Gilbert Roland /
Luis Antonio Damaso de Alonso**

1905 - 1994

Mexico

Known as "The Puerto Rican Pepper Pot" she was typically cast as gorgeous Latina spitfires throughout her Hollywood career. Active in film during the 1940s, in 1946 she got her first major screen role in the movie *Blue Skies*, getting billed alongside the likes of Bing Crosby, Fred Astaire, Joan Caulfield and Billy De Wolfe. With a successful career in Hollywood's musicals and comedies, other credits include the blockbusters *The Beautiful Blonde from Bashful Bend*, *One Touch of Venus* and *Variety Girl*. Born and raised in Brooklyn, Olga San Juan started out performing on the radio. Besides being a talented actress Olga was also an accomplished dancer and comic, who married film star Edmond O'Brien.

Olga San Juan
1927-

USA

Sheen has been nominated for twelve Emmy Awards, winning three, earned eight nominations for Golden Globe Awards and has a star on the Hollywood Walk of Fame, at 1500 Vine Street. He has played U.S. President John F. Kennedy, Attorney General Robert Kennedy, White House Chief of Staff A.J. McInnerney, sinister future president Greg Stillson in *The Dead Zone*, and fictional democratic president Josiah Bartlet in the acclaimed television drama *The West Wing*, but he is best known for his role as Captain Willard in the film *Apocalypse Now*. Of Galician-Irish descent, Sheen had wanted to act since he was very young, to his father's disapproval. In spite of this, Sheen borrowed money from a priest and headed to New York City where, greatly influenced by the actor James Dean, he developed a theater company with other actors in hopes that a production would earn him recognition. In 1974, Sheen portrayed a hot rod driver in the TV movie *The California Kid*, and that same year received an Emmy Award nomination for Best Actor in a television drama for his portrayal of Pvt. Eddie Slovik in the made-for-television film, *The Execution of Private Slovik*. It is said that his performance in this film led director Francis Ford Coppola to choose him for the starring role in *Apocalypse Now*, which gained him wide recognition.

**Martin Sheen /
Ramón Gerardo Antonio Estévez**
1940

USA

Born in Oaxaca, Mexico, Lupita Tovar appeared first in Fox silent films before making the move to Universal and co-starring in the Spanish-language version of 1930's *The Cat Creeps* (La Voluntad del Muerto). For the same producer, Czech-born Paul Kohner, she appeared as Eva (the Spanish-language counterpart of Helen Chandler's Mina) in Universal's *Spanish Dracula*. In 1932, she married Kohner, who later became one of the top agents in Hollywood. (Their actress-daughter Susan Kohner was Oscar-nominated for her performance in Universal's 1959 *Imitation of Life,* and their son Pancho Kohner is a Hollywood producer) Tovar gave up films in the 1940s and has been widowed since 1988.

Lupita Tovar
1911

Mexico

The life of actress Lupe Vélez is the stuff legends are made of. Some sources say that she was the daughter of a prostitute and was sent to Texas at the age of 13 to live in a convent, but she wasn't much of a student because she was "so rambunctious." Life was hard, and Lupe returned to Mexico to help her family out financially. In 1924, Lupe started her career on the Mexican stage, wowing audiences with her natural beauty and talent. By 1927, she had migrated to Hollywood, where she was discovered by Hal Roach, who cast her in a comedy with Stan Laurel and Oliver Hardy (El Gordo y el Flaco). After two bit parts, she got the lead in *The Gaucho* with Douglas Fairbanks, Sr. Her Hollywood career is considered the most successful of all Mexican stars of that age. She didn't have any trouble making the transition from silent films to talkies, and her most memorable films are those from the *Mexican Spitfire* series of the late 1930s. Audiences loved her for her madcap adventures, but it seemed at times she was better known for her stormy love affairs. She was a big Hollywood star, yet she happened to be very unlucky in love. She married one of her lovers, Johnny Weissmuller, the Tarzan of that era, an affair that only lasted five years and was filled with battles, she then had a failed romance with Gary Cooper, who never wanted to wed her. Tired of yet another failed romance with Harald Maresch and pregnant with his child, Lupe committed suicide with an overdose of Seconal. She was only 36 years old.

**Lupe Vélez /
María Guadalupe Vélez de Villalobos**
1908 - 1944

Mexico

When Benicio Del Toro, the young Puerto Rican thespian, walked away with an Academy Award for best supporting actor for his performance in the movie *Traffic* in 2001, at first glance it did not seem like a major breakthrough for Latinos in Hollywood. José Ferrer, a fellow Puerto Rican, won the Best Actor Award many decades before for his interpretation of *Cyrano De Bergerac,* and actress, singer and dancer Rita Moreno, also a multitalented Puerto Rican, won a Best Supporting Actress Award for her work in *West Side Story*. However, Del Toro's recognition definitely marks a first in the history of Latinos in film: The winning portrayal was for a character who spoke only in Spanish, a landmark for Hispanics in the movie mecca, and a feat achieved only once before, back in 1975 in the second part of the *Godfather* saga, with the great Robert DeNiro speaking in Italian.

And when the Colombian actress Catalina Sandino Moreno got her chance to stroll down the red carpet as one of the Oscar nominees for best actress in 2005, again not a first for a Latina, the film in which she played the nominated role, *Maria Full of Grace* (*María llena de gracia*), was a movie made entirely in Spanish, filmed mostly in Colombia and considered a foreign language film by Hollywood standards. That same year, *Al Otro Lado Del Río*, a song by Uruguayan composer Jorge Drexler featured in the Walter Salles film *Motorcycle Diaries* (*Diarios de Motocicleta*) became the first song in Spanish to win an Oscar (this was the second win for a song in

The galaxy of Latino stars in the wide and ever-expanding Big Bang that is Hollywood's universe is populated today by all kinds of performers.

Actress, singer and dancer Rita Moreno won a Best Supporting Actress Award for her work in the 1961 musical West Side Story.

a language other than English, the first was given way back in 1962 to *Ta paidia toy Peiraia* [*Children of Piraeus*], by Greek composer Manos Hadjidakis featured in the film *Never on Sunday)*. José Rivera, hired to write the screenplay for *Motorcycle Diaries*, became the first Hispanic to be nominated by the Academy for best adapted screenplay for a film spoken in Spanish and Quechua.

Guillermo Del Toro, Alejandro González Iñárritu and Alfonso Cuarón, three talented Mexican directors, have inserted their unique movie making style into the Hollywood mainstream, gaining accolades and recognition in the international arena for their respective projects, all major blockbuster hits and most of them also done in Spanish.

The galaxy of Latino stars in the wide and ever-expanding Big Bang that is Hollywood's universe is populated today by all kinds of performers: Veterans like Edward James Olmos, star of films like *Stand and Deliver*, *America Me* and *Mi Familia*, as well as TV series like *Miami Vice* and *Batlestar Galactica*, and 1970s comedian Richard "Cheech" Marín of *Up in Smoke* fame, who was a regular on the television series *Nash Bridges*, starred in and directed his own feature film *Born in East L.A.*, has also appeared in numerous other movies and television shows.

Ricardo Montalbán, who during the 50s and 60s was one of the few working Hispanic actors in Hollywood, and has appeared in a variety of films and television projects, and still remains a constant figure. Credited in movies like *The Naked Gun* and two of the *Planet of the Apes* series films, as well as appearing in the second and third *Spy Kids* films as the kids' grandfather, the actor was born in Mexico City, the offspring of Spanish parents.

His real name is Ricardo Gonzalo Pedro Montalbán Merino. His role in the television series *Fantasy Island* from 1978 to 1984 as the ethnically ambiguous Mr. Roarke gave Montalbán worldwide

Hervé Villechaize and Ricardo Montalbán greet visitors in the television series Fantasy Island.

recognition. His portrayal of villain Khan Noonien Singh in *Star Trek II: The Wrath of Khan*, a role he reprised from a 1967 episode of Star Trek called "Space Seed," made him a science fiction favorite, and his Chrysler Cordoba commercials made him famous as the "Corinthian leather" guy, many times parodied and equally iconic. His commitment to changing the image of Hispanics in Hollywood, led to the fall of the "Frito Bandido" commercials on television and the formation of NOSOTROS.

His portrayal of villain Khan Noonien Singh in Star Trek II: The Wrath of Khan, a role he reprised from a 1967 episode of Star Trek called "Space Seed," (at left) made of star Ricardo Montalbán a science fiction favorite.

Laurence Fishburne and Andy García in a scene from Hoodlum (1997).

Andy García, born Andrés Arturo García Menéndez in Havana, Cuba, is also an established big star in the Hollywood constellation. His break came when he was given a role as a gang member in the first episode of the popular TV series *Hill Street Blues*. The part of a sharp-shooting, short-fused Italian cop in the blockbuster *The Untouchables* made García a popular Hollywood actor, and his portrayal of the illegitimate son of Sonny Corleone in *The Godfather: Part III* earned the actor an Academy Award nomination as best supporting actor. His performance made him an internationally acclaimed star. Recently he also appeared in the remake of *Ocean's Eleven* alongside many of today's biggest stars. In 2006 he made his directing debut with a project he had been nurturing for over 15 years. Working with a script from famed Cuban screenwriter and novelist Gillermo Cabrera Infante, known in Hollywood as Guillermo Cain (the author of the screenplay for the famous 1971 film *Vanishing Point* as well as the 1997 made-for-television movie of the same title), García was at the helm and in front of the lens in *The Lost City*, a drama set in 1950s pre-revolutionary Cuba.

An accomplished guitarist, singer and dancer, Héctor Elizondo was discovered at age 10 by the legendary W.C. Handy and appeared with him on local radio and TV. Born in West Harlem of a Basque father and a Puerto Rican mother, he was quite an athlete, his high school baseball skills were so good that he was scouted by the Pittsburgh Pirates. Elizondo has an impressive body of work, with over 120 film and television projects under his belt. His performances in the dramatic television series *Chicago Hope* during the early nineties earned him several acting nominations and as many awards and recognitions. A favorite of famed director Garry Marshall, he has worked in 12 of his movies, appearing with both Richard Gere and Julia Roberts in *Pretty Woman*, for which he received a Golden Globe Award nomination for best supporting actor, and in *Runaway Bride*.

Best known for his role in the film *Apocalypse Now* and, most recently, as President Josiah Bartlet on the acclaimed television drama *The West Wing*, Martin Sheen is of Latino descent but has never played a Latino in film. Sheen was born in Dayton, Ohio, to a Spanish-born father and an Irish mother, and his real name is Ramón Gerardo Antonio Estévez. He has enjoyed a long, successful acting career while holding on to his Hollywood star status. A Hollywood legacy of sorts, the Sheen brothers (or the Estévez brothers), his sons, have also reached Hollywood stardom, relying heavily on their own talent. Members of the 1980s Brat-pack phenomena, both Charlie Sheen, who obviously preferred to stick with his father's Hollywood moniker, and Emilio Estévez, the clear-eyed heartthrob of John Hughes' *The Breakfast Club*, and the director of the critically-acclaimed political drama *Bobby* released in 2006, are keeping very busy, both on, as well as off-camera, while enjoying their respective stardom.

To avid trekkies Perry López is best remembered as Esteban Rodríguez, a Starfleet botanist serving aboard the USS Enterprise in the *Star Trek* episode titled "Shore Leave," but to everybody else the talented actor of Puerto Rican descent is best known for his performance as police officer Lou Escobar in Roman Polanski's *Chinatown* (1974), a part López reprised (his character now promoted to captain) in the 1990 sequel titled *The Two Jakes*. Described as a "tough-talking American character actor" the New York-born López made his stage debut in the early 1950s and then signed a contract with Warner Bros. which led the actor to work in such films such as *Mister Roberts* (1955), *The McConnell Story* (1956) and *The Violent Road* (1958). A very busy Hollywood artist, López's credit appears in well over 70 film and television projects, working alongside the likes of Charles Bronson, Henry Fonda, James Cagney and, of course, Jack Nicholson.

Above: From the left, Dennis Hopper, Martin Sheen and Frederic Forrest in a scene from Francis Ford Coppola's Apocalypse Now.

At left: To trekkies around the globe Perry López is best remembered as Esteban Rodríguez, a Starfleet botanist aboard the USS Enterprise.

Above: From the left, Richard Bakalyan, Perry López as Lieutenant Lou Escobar and Jack Nicholson in Cinatown *(1974).*

At right: Character actor Ismael "East" Carlo.

Renee Victor, Ramón Franco, Elizabeth Peña, Henry Silva and Miguel Sandoval are also part of this group of screen professionals. While not in the same category of movie stars who dominate the box office, these artists remain equally strong in both leading and supporting parts, oftentimes playing roles outside the typical Latino type-casting.

The regular supporting Latinos on screen are mainly played by the likes of Puerto Rican actor Ismael "East" Carlo who is sometimes credited as either East Carlo, Ismael East Carlo, Ismael Carlo or Ismael De Carlo and has appeared in more than 80 films. Or Henry Darrow (born Henry Thomas Delgado and of Puerto Rican descent) who has over 120 titles to his credit.

Above: Luis Guzmán

Below: Jimmy Smits

Facing page film strip: In Memoriam from the top, René Henriquez, Alex Colón and poet Miguel Piñero.

Also a versatile and very busy contemporary character actor is the brilliant Puerto Rican performer Luis Guzmán. Born in Cayey, Puerto Rico, Guzmán possesses a long and distinguished acting career, both in film and television. He was Jacopo in the latest version of *The Count of Monte Cristo*, played the part of Pachanga in *Carlito's Way* opposite Al Pacino, and is a favorite of Academy Award-winning directors Steven Soderbergh and Paul Thomas Anderson.

Film and television actor Jimmy Smits, born to a Surinamese father and a Puerto Rican mother, is a Golden Globe and Emmy winner who can be seen in the *Star Wars* films and such television programs as the popular *Miami Vice*, *NYPD Blue*, *L.A. Law* and the most recent *The West Wing* where he played a congressman from Texas who becomes President of the United States as the series ended in 2006. He was arrested for his participation in protests against U.S. Navy bombings practices in the Puerto Rican offshore island of Vieques, and since 1986 has been in a relationship with the wonderful actress Wanda de Jesús, who can also be seen on dozens of television shows and such films as *Blood Work* with Clint Eastwood and her latest, *Illegal Tender*, released in 2007.

Gone, yet not forgotten, are character actors René Enríquez, who began his film career in Woody Allen's hilarious comedy *Bananas* and who enjoyed a long and productive career in television, including *Hill Street Blues*; Alex Colón, who began his stage acting career on Broadway in Neil Simon's drama *The Gingerbread Lady* in 1970 and immediately thereafter his film and television career took off and he appeared in over 25 motion pictures and hundreds of television shows; and the controversial, but undeniably talented playwright, poet and performer Miguel Piñero, most famous for writing *Short Eyes*. They are gone, yet they are still a constant presence, thanks to the magic of the moving image, the closest thing to immortality we know.

Actors like Tony Plana, of television's *Ugly Betty*, Eric Estrada, who is now enjoying a comeback thanks to the reality television phenomena, Lorenzo Lamas, Jaime Sánchez, Carlos Rivas, James Victor, John Scott Urena, Santos Morales, John Vargas and Efraín Figueroa, are also part of a hard-working elite of Latino performers keeping the torch lit and paving the way for all newcomers. Or actresses like Raquel Welch, Venezuelan beauty María Conchita Alonso; character actress Lupe Ontiveros, the fiery Rosie Pérez and the talented Rachel Ticotin, hard at work and reaping the fruits of their efforts, or Linda Cristal, a glorious and talented beauty during her heyday and now retired from the screen in her native Argentina; they all have garnered a respectable position in Hollywood with their work.

Above: Raquel Welch, a 60s sex symbol of Bolivian descent, steals the scene.

Below: Henry plays a Puerto Rican Cop in Contract on Cherry Street

Luis Valdez, often credited for opening doors for Hispanics in 1980 with the now-classic *Zoot Suit*, an Edward James Olmos vehicle, in 1987 wrote and directed *La Bamba*, the story of tragic 1950s singer Ricardo Valenzuela, better known as young rebel and early rocker, Richie Valens. This box office hit starred Lou Diamond Phillips and Esaí Morales, in a role that is considered by many to be Morales' best.

Producer Montezuma Esparza first made a name for himself in the 1980s with *Gettysburg*, *The Battle of Gregorio Cortez* and *The Milagro Beanfield War*, a film starring singer Rubén Blades. He then went on to produce the blockbuster *Selena*, a biopic about the popular and violently slain singer of Mexican descent, which was Jennifer López's first major role.

Mexican actor and director Alfonso Arau, who directed *Like Water for Chocolate*, at the time the highest grossing foreign film in the United States, and Gregory Nava, who received an Oscar nomination for best foreign language film for *El Norte* and who wrote and directed *Mi Familia* are still contributing to the cause.

Jacobo Morales, the Puerto Rican actor and director and Academy Award nominee for best foreign language film for *Lo que el paso a Santiago* (*Santiago, the Story of His New Life*), who every so often regales us with a memorable and Caribbean flavored piece of "dramedy," is still active and productive in the Puerto Rican movie and television industries. He was also wonderfully funny in Woody Allen's *Bananas*.

Robert Rodríguez, a young Texas writer, director, editor, music composer and all-around renaissance man of Mexican descent, is already a staple of the movie-making world with two popular franchises under his belt, *El Mariachi* and *Spy Kids*, both highlighting Latino culture and featuring mostly Latino characters. In 2007 he joined with action director Quentin Tarantino to make *Grindhouse*, a double feature within the same movie.

Salma Hayek, Gael García Bernal, Eva Méndez, John Leguizamo, Jennifer López and her husband Marc Anthony (an entertainment industry power couple), Roselín Sánchez, Benjamin Bratt, Eva Longoria, Penélope Cruz, Antonio Banderas, Cameron Díaz, newcomers Michelle Rodríguez of *Girl Fight* and *Lost* fame, Víctor Rasuk the young star of *Raising Víctor Vargas*, the handsome Jay Hernández, main character in Eli Roth's slasher fest *Hostel*, and the up and coming Adam Rodríguez, star of television's *CSI: Miami*, the list of contemporary Latino talent goes on and on.

Currently a TV family sitcom stars George López, as a Mexican-American dad and the head of a dysfunctional Latino family circle (Mexican immigrant mother, Cuban father-in-law). And there is Sister Peter Marie Reimondo, the role played by Rita Moreno, on *Oz*, and Freddy Rodríguez as Federico Díaz on *Six Feet Under*. *Survivor*, *24*, *Lost* and *Desperate Housewives*, all major network hits, have Latinos billed among their main cast members. *Dora the Explorer*, and the charismatic Diego, *Taína*, and the wrestlers of the Saturday morning cartoon show *Mucha Lucha* are all Latino characters (as well as children's favorites) and featured in programs promoting cultural variety and bilingual education, while at the same time displaying the mores, traditions and diversity of the Latino population. The "telenovelas" are the latest rage with *Betty La Fea* being done in English (*Ugly Betty*). Plus América Ferrara, the protagonist of the new version, winning the coveted Emmy Award for best actress in a television comedy just makes everything more vivid. Even former Miss Universe, Puerto Rican Dayanara Torres, gets top billing in the American television dramatic series *Watch Over Me*.

At Top: Argentinian born pianist, conductor and composer Lalo Schifrin, here in concert with the Big Band of the Kölner Musikhochschule, has written over 100 scores for both television and the cinema. During his illustrious career, he has received four Grammy Awards and has been nominated for the Oscar in six occasions.

At Right: Javier Bardem in Love in the Time of Cholera, *based on a novel by Gabriel García Márquez.*

Facing page: Actor/director Alfonso Arau, Kathleen Turner and Michael Douglas in Romancing the Stone *(1984).*

From the top: Scene from El Cantante. *Promo art for the animated series* ¡Mucha Lucha! *Ramón Franco during the filming of the television series* Tour of Duty *(1987). John Leguizamo during a screening.*

Javier Bardem, a young Spanish actor, is taking the big screen by storm with powerful performances that spark Oscar buzz all over the media. Be it playing an irrepressible lovestruck romantic in Gabriel García Márquez's *Love in The Times of Cholera* or a ruthless cold-blooded killer in the Coen Brothers film *No Country for Old Men*, he is without doubt a strong presence in modern-day Hollywood.

And that is just the actors and actresses, the pretty and appealing faces up on screen, alongside the upper tier of the movie-making world. There are also many Latinos working behind the scenes. This rising presence of Hispanics in mainstream Hollywood not only responds to a demographic reality, with Latinos listed as the largest nonwhite ethnic group according to the latest census figures in the United States, it also shows the steps taken by the new generation of Latino stars and movie makers, to claim a well-deserved space in this important and complicated media outlet.

But despite this reality, the Hollywood moviemaking structure still denies the Latino population a just amount of representation, be it (unbelievable as it may sound) onscreen or at the executive level. According to the latest industry reports: the majority of Hollywood roles are reserved for Anglos. Although Hispanics represent a large percentage of the U.S. population at 47 million (14% and growing), in the period reported by the Screen Actors' Guild (SAG) (2006), out of approximately 53,000 roles available for casting, a mere 2,600 (4.9 %) were actually offered to Latino actors. The union does report, however, an increase in the number of parts offered to Latinos and other minorities during this period. Yet this growth does

From the top: Gael García Bernal shares a moment with his fans. Antonio Banderas is El Mariachi. *A scene from* Raising Víctor Vargas, *a Víctor Rasuk vehicle. América Ferrara, a sure winner.*

not reflect the realities of the presence of Latinos and other minorities in modern society and the parts offered do not make a believable effort to portray in a positive light the contributions of these respective groups to American culture.

There is a noticeable lack of Hispanic casting agents, development and other upper-level movie executives within the studio system. Hollywood is in dire need of more writers, producers and artists willing to put on the big screen an accurate portrayal of real Latino lifestyles.

And then again, how much has Hollywood really changed when portraying Latinos on film? Yes, Jennifer López gets to kiss and to keep the guy, but she was a *Maid in Manhattan*, and *Carlito's Way* is still the way of the cheap street mafiosi and the ultra mucho macho violence, also represented by John Leguizamo's role in *Empire*. Sadly, Hispanics, despite their growing number of roles, on screen presence and recognition, are still predominantly playing the part of the gardener or the maid, the hot señorita, the ruthless gangster or, even worse, the "no habla inglés" leaf blower operator, submissive sweatshop worker, street corner whore, anonymous henchmen and street thug.

However, there are Latinos leaving an indelible and positive mark throughout the Hollywood landscape. Their valuable contribution not only honors those romantic figures of yore, the famous Latinos of the early days of filmmaking, it also pays homage to those who persistently labor to feature on screen the many dimensions of Hispanics, a noble heritage well deserving of being properly addressed and fully appreciated.

Bibliography

Adams, Les & Buck Rainey, Shoot-Em-Ups, Arlington House Publishing, 1978.

Anger, Kenneth, Hollywood Babylon, Bell Publishing Co., New York, 1981.

Baxter, John, Sixty Years of Hollywood, A. S. Barnes & Company & The Tantivity Press, 1973

Blum, Daniel, Screen World, Biblo & Tannen Booksellers & Publishers, 1956

Clarke, John Engstead, Star Shots: 50 Years of Pictures & Stories, Irwin & Company, 1978

Cowie, Peter, Seventy Years of Cinema, Castle Books, New York, 1969

Dolan, Edward F., Jr., History of the Movies, Bison Book Corp., 1983

Douglas Eames, John, The MGM Story, Crown Publisher, Inc. 1976

Douglas Eames, John, The Paramount Story, Octopus Books Limited, 1985

Fox Sheinwold, Patricia, Gone But Not Forgotten, Bell Publishing Company, MCMLXXXII

Gelman, Barbara, Mountain of Dreams, Photoplay Treasury, Macfadden Bartell Corporation & Crown Publishers Of New York, 1972

Greenfield, Jeff, Television: The First Fifty Years, Harry N. Abrams, Inc., 1977

Hadley-García, George, Hispanic Hollywood: The Latins in Motion Pictures, Carol Publishing Group, 1990

Halliwell, Leslie, The Filmgoer's Companion, Hoill & Wang New York, 1965, 1967, 1970, 1974, 1976, 1977

Halliwell, Leslie, The Golden Years of Paramount Pictures, Stonehill Publishing Company, 1976

Hirschhorn, Clive, The Universal Story, Crown Publishing, Inc., Octopus Books Limited, New York, 1983

Hirschhorn, Clive, The Warner Bros. Story, Crown Publishing, Inc., New York, 1979

Hover, Ronald, Hollywood, Alfred D. Knopf, Inc., 1960

Hyams, Jay, The Life and Times of the Western Movie, Gallery Books, New York, 1983

Jewel, Richard B. & Vernon Harbin, The RKO Story, Arlington House, Div. of Crown Publishing, 1982

Katz, Ephraim, The Film Encyclopedia, Thomas Y. Crowell Publishers, 1979

Keylin, Arleen, ed., The Forties: As Reported by: The NY Times, Arno Press Inc. 1980

Kidd, Charles, Debrett Goes to Hollywood, St. Martin's Press, New York, 1986

Leish, Kenneth W., A History of Cinema, Newsweek Books, New York, 1974

Marrill, Alvin H., The Films of Anthony Quinn, Citadel Press, 1975

Medved, Harry & Michael, The Golden Turkey Awards, G.P. Putnam's Sons, 1980

Medved, Harry & Randy Freyfuss, The Black Performer in Motion Pictures: The Fifty Worst Films of All Time and How they Got that Way, Popular Library, 1978

Meyer, Nicholas E., Magic in the Dark: A Young Viewer's History Of the Movies, Facts on File Publications, New York, New York, 1985

Michael, Paul, The Academy Awards, (A Pictorial History), Crown Publishers, Inc., New York 1964, 1968, 1972, 1975, 1978

Mill, Gary, Black Hollywood, Citadel Press, 1975

Montalbán, Ricardo with Bob Thomas, Reflections: A Life in Two Worlds, Doubleday & Company, Inc., Garden City, NY, 1980

Parise, James Robert & Don E. Stanke, The All-Americans, Arlington House, 1977

Parish, James Robert, Hollywood Character Actors, Arlington House Publisher, 1977

Pascall, Jeremy, Fifty Years of Movies: Illustrated History of Motion Pictures from 1930 to the Present, The Hamlyn Publishing Group, Ltd., 1981

Pickard, Roy, The Hollywood Story: The Complete History of 50 Roaring Years, Chartwell Book, Inc., 1986

Pinto, Alfonso, Hollywood's Spanish-Language Films: A Neglected Chapter of the American Cinema, 1930-1935, Films in Review, Oct. 1973, Vol. XXIV No. 8, pages 474-483

Quigley, Martin, Jr. and Richard Gertner, Films in America: A Panoramic View of Four Decades, Western Publishing Company, 1970

Ringgold, Gene, The Films of Rita Hayworth, Citadel Press, Secaucus, New Jersey, 1974

Reyes Luis and Peter Rubie, Hispanics in Hollywood: A Celebration of 100 Years in Film and Television, Lone Eagle Publishing Co. 2000

Springer, John & Jack Hamilton, They Had Faces Then, Super Stars, Stars & Starlets of the 1930's, Citadel Press, Secaucus, New Jersey, 1974

Thomas, Tony, & Audrey Solomon, The Film of 20th Century Fox: A Pictorial History, Citadel Press, 1979

Wilkersen, Tichi & Marcia Borie, Hollywood Legends: The Golden Years of the Hollywood Reporter, Tale/Weaver Publishing, Inc., 1988

Zinman, David, 50 Classic Motion Pictures: The Stuff That Dreams Are Made of, A selection of Vintage Films from Hollywood's Golden Age, Chelsea House, 1983

Zinman, David, 50 from the 50's: Vintage Films from America's mid-century, Arlington House, 1979

Image Index

Note: All vintage images are public domain unless noted otherwise. All images are the sole property of their respective owners and are used under the fair use clause of the 1976 Copyright Act. Thanks to the Bison Archives and Mr. Marc Wanamaker for the access to their image collection.

Page 1 Façade "Hollywood... Se Habla Español"
Page 2-3 Collage 1: "Hall of Fame"
Page 5 Duncan Renaldo
Page 7 Lupe Vélez
Page 8 Little Rascals
Page 12 Ricardo Montalbán
Page 15 Duncan Renaldo
Page 17 Poster art for Maré Nostrum
Page 19 Dolores Del Río
Page 20 The Night is Young
Page 21 Vicente Blasco Ibáñez
Page 22 Her Husband's Secret
Page 23, 24 Dolores Del Río
Page 26, 27 and 28 Lupe Vélez
Page 31 Cover of "Photoplay"
Page 32 Greta Garbo and Antonio Moreno
Page 33 Rudolph Valentino
Page 34 Mauritz Stiller (left) directs Greta Garbo and Antonio Moreno.
Page 35-36 Antonio Moreno
Page 37 Poster art for The Temptress
Page 38 Dolores Del Río
Page 39 Ramón Novarro
Page 40 Ben Hur
Page 41 Poster art for Scaramouche
Page 42-43 Ramón Novarro
Page 45 Don Alvarado, Pedro de Córdoba
Page 46 Duncan Renaldo
Page 47 Fernando Lamas and Gilbert Roland
Page 48 Poster art for New York Night
Page 49 What a Night
Page 50 Poster art for The Son of the Sheik
Page 51 Ricardo Cortez
Page 53 The complete cast of The Cat and the Canary (La Voluntad del Muerto)
Page 55 Rita Hayworth
Page 56 Poster art for Rio Rita
Page 57 Rio Rita
Page 58 Buster Keaton
Page 59 Xavier Cugat
Page 60 Cuesta Abajo
Page 61 Lupita Tovar and Antonio Moreno
Page 63 Mexican bandit leader Pancho Villa, c1916. National Archives and Records Administration
Page 64 Vaquero
Page 65 Las Norias Bandit Raid: Texas Rangers with dead bandits, October 8, 1915
The Robert Runyon Photograph Collection, courtesy of The Center for American History, The University of Texas at Austin.
Page 66 William S. Hart
Page 67 Mexican boy with guitar
Page 68 Pancho Villa
Page 71 Alfonso Bedoya
Page 72 Crispín Martin
Page 73 Katy Jurado
Page 74 Katy Jurado and Ernest Borgnine
Page 75 Anthony Quinn
Page 76 Cisco Kid
Page 77 Poster art for The Cisco Kid
Page 79 Guy Williams as Zorro
Page 80 Nahl's earliest image of a Joaquín Murrieta, Mountain Bandit
Page 81 Cover art for El Zorro
Page 85 top to bottom: Cantinflas / Anthony Quinn / José ferrer / Lady of Shanghai / Black Lagoon
Page 86 Pedro Almendáriz and Carlos López

Moctezuma / Pedro Armendáriz
Page 87 Cuban Pete/Desi Arnaz
Page 88 Rudy Acosta and Elvis Presley in Flaming Star / Rudy Acosta
Page 89 Don Alvarado
Page 90 The Treasure of the Sierra Madre / Alfonso Bedoya
Page 91 Blackboard Jungle / Rafael Campos
Page 92 Leo Carrillo
Page 93 Miriam Colón Valle / Scarface
Page 94 Francisco Álvarez and Mapy Cortés in Al marido hay que seguirlo / Mapy Cortés
Page 95 Self-caricature by Xavier Cugat / Xavier Cugat and his band
Page 96 The Flirt (1917) - Harold Lloyd, Bebe Daniels / Bebe Daniels
Page 97 Dorothy Patrick, Arturo de Córdova, Louis Armstrong, Billie Holiday, and other musicians in New Orleans / Arturo de Córdova
Page 98 What Price Glory / Dolores Del Río
Page 99 Raising Helen / Héctor Elizondo
Page 100 José Ferrer
Page 101 Thomas Gómez / Ride the Pink Horse
Page 102 Gilda / Rita Hayworth
Page 103 Juano Hernández
Page 104 Kiss of the Spider Woman / Raúl Juliá
Page 105 Katy Jurado / Arthur Kennedy, Katy Jurado and Glenn Ford
Page 106 Dangerous When Wet / Fernando Lamas
Page 107 Perry López c. 1956 / Chinatown
Page 108 The cast of Cuesta Abajo / Mona Maris
Page 109 Carmen Miranda
Page 110 Ricardo Montalbán
Page 111 Cobra Woman / María Montes
Page 112 Sara Montiel
Page 113 Original still from Mare Nostrum. Madame Paquereet as Dr. Fedelmann, Antonio Moreno as Ulysses Ferragut and Alice Terry as Freya Talberg / Antonio Moreno
Page 114 Around The World in 80 Days / Mario Moreno Cantinflas
Page 115 West Side Story (United Artists Corporation) / Rita Moreno
Page 116 Ramón Novarro (right) with Francis Xavier Bushman in Ben-Hur / Ramón Novarro
Page 117 Blade Runner / Edward James Olmos
Page 118 Anthony Quinn
Page 119 Peter Lorre and Duncan Renaldo (from the collection of Stephen Youngkin) / Duncan Renaldo as Cisco Kid
Page 120 Alejandro Rey
Page 121 Fernando Rey (left) in Le Charme discret de la bourgeoisie / Fernando Rey
Page 122 César Romero
Page 123 Gilbert Roland
Page 124 Olga San Juan and Bob Hope / Olga San Juan
Page 125 Martin Sheen / Apocalypse Now
Page 126 Dracula / Lupita Tovar
Page 127 Lupe Vélez and Gary Cooper in Wolf Song / Lupe Vélez
Page 131 West Side Story
Page 132 Ricardo Montalbán Fantasy Island and Star Trek (TV series)
Page 133 Hoodlum
Page 134 Apocalypse Now / Perry López
Page 135 Chinatown / Ismael Carlo
Page 136 Luis Guzmán / Jimmy Smits
Page 137 René Enríques / Alex Colón / Miguel Piñero / Raquel Welch / Henry Silva
Page 138 Romancing the Stone
Page 139 Javier Bardem / Lalo Schifrin, photo by Alexandra Spürk (Alexi) licensed under the Creative Commons Attribution ShareAlike 2.5 License.
Page 140 El Cantante / ¡Mucha Lucha! / Tour of Duty / John Leguizamo
Page 141 Gael García Bernal / El Mariachi / Raising Víctor Vargas / América Ferrara
Pages 148-149 Collage 2 "Today and Tomorrow"

1. César Romero
2. Nan Leslie, Nick Adams, Natalie Wood and Perry López. c. 1956
3. A young Duncan Renaldo, at right with boomerang.
4. Beau Bridges and José Ferrer
5. Anthony Quinn and Dolores Del Río
6. Woody Strode and Peter Finch in a scene from the movie *The Sins of Rachel Cade* in which Juano Hernández (at center) plays Kalanumu.
7. Robert Young, Carmen Miranda and William Holden
8. Raquel Welch
9. Pedro Almendáriz and Carlos López Monctezuma
10. Rita Hayworth and George Macready in a scene from *Gilda*.
11. Thomas Gómez
12. Mario Moreno "Cantinflas" and Jimmy Durante during a scene of *Pepe*.
13. Ricardo Montalbán (center) with part of the cast of the Flying Nun.
14. Promo photo from *The Four Horsemen of Apocalypse*

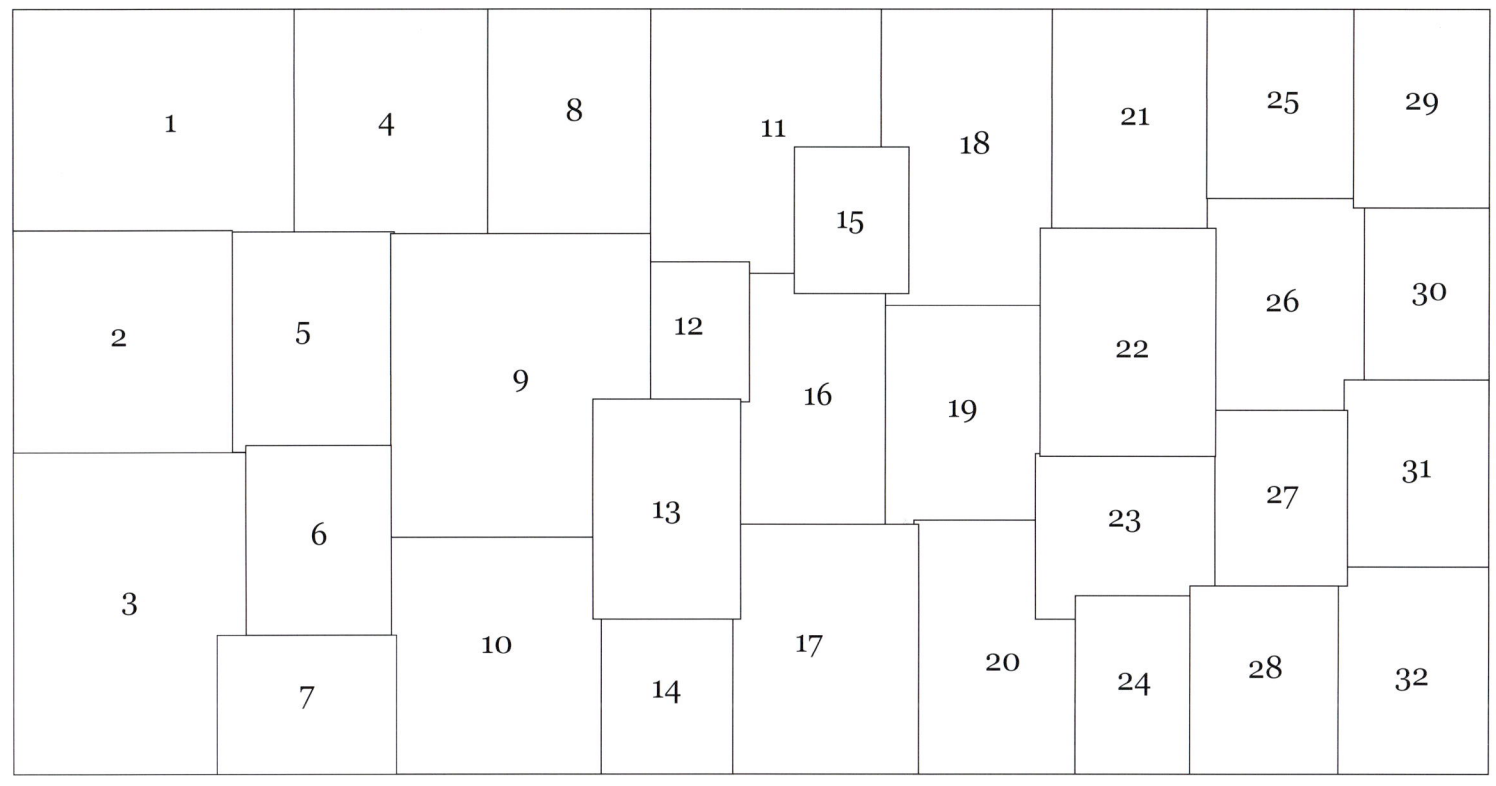

1. Eva Longoria - Mexican descent
2. Salma Hayek - Mexico
3. Penélope Cruz - Spain
4. James Víctor - Dominican descent
5. Eric Estrada - Puerto Rican descent
6. Efraín Figueroa - Puerto Rican descent
7. Linda Kristal - Argentina
8. Jay Hernández - Mexican descent
9. Lupe Ontiveros and America Ferrara - Mexican descent
10. Eva Méndez - Cuban descent
11. Michelle Rodríguez - Puerto Rican - Dominican descent
12. Fernando Allende - Mexico
13. Roselín Sánchez - Puerto Rico
14. Diego Luna - Mexico
15. Richard "Cheech" Marín - Mexican descent
16. Isela Vega - Mexico
17. Ramón Sandoval - Mexican descent
18. Esaí Morales - Puerto Rico
19. John Vargas - Puerto Rican descent
20. Rosie Pérez - Puerto Rican descent
21. Henry Darrow - Puerto Rican descent
22. Talissa Soto - Puerto Rico
23. Frankie Muñiz - Puerto Rican descent
24. Lillian Hurst - Puerto Rico
25. Modesto Lacén - Puerto Rico
26. George López - Mexican descent
27. William Márquez - Cuba
28. Lorenzo Lamas - Argentine descent
29. Cameron Díaz - Cuban descent
30. Adam Rodríguez - Cuban - Puerto Rican descent
31. Benjamín Bratt - Peruvian descent
32. Wanda De Jesús - Puerto Rico